GW00865230

Spreading Our Wings

Words Alive

Words Alive

Original title
Spreading Our Wings

Cover image
Whooper Swans by Christine Cassidy

Cover design
Sonja Smolec

Layout and edit
Sonja Smolec
Yossi Faybish

Published by
Aquillrelle

Copyright 2017
All rights reserved - © Words Alive

No part of this book may be reproduced or transmitted in any form or by any means, graphic, electronic, or mechanical, including photocopying, recording, taping, or by any information storage retrieval system, without the permission, in writing, from the publisher.

ISBN 978-1-326-97544-9

Acknowledgments

Words Alive Writing Group gratefully acknowledges the financial assistance and support of Engage with Age and The Big Lottery Fund's Awards for All Northern Ireland programme. The group also extends a big thank you to all the participants and the staff who have made us welcome in their various venues as part of our Outreach Project. Grateful thanks to Christine Cassidy and Lindsay Hodges for the cover image and note, respectively. And thank you also to Donegall Pass Community Centre and staff for kindly giving the group houseroom.

Words Alive
https://sites.google.com/site/wordsalivebelfast79/home
wordsalivebelfast79@gmail.com

Engage With Age
http://www.engagewithage.org.uk/

The Big Lottery Fund
http://www.biglotteryfund.org.uk/

Cover image: Whooper Swans by Christine Cassidy,
In Touch With The Wild Photography
https://www.facebook.com/InTouchWithTheWildByChristineCassidy/

A note on Whooper Swans

In late Autumn every year, Whooper Swans from Iceland begin their strenuous flight to overwinter in Northern Ireland, their knowledge of our habitat seemingly passed down from generation to generation and learnt as they fly in family groups in their distinctive V shape.

The incredible journey these birds make to reach us cannot be underestimated, the longest flight distance of any swan, some 800-1,400 km between Britain/Ireland and Iceland. On arrival the sound is phenomenal, as the swans greet and acknowledge each other with noisy whoops that explain their name. They are celebrating – happy to have survived the crossing and excited that their friends and neighbours have also touched down safely.

For these enigmatic birds, there is both comfort and strength in company. The life of Whooper Swans is to reach out together for pastures new as well as returning to familiar places. It is all a question of choosing the moment – at the right time and by instinct, they know when to go and why. They just spread their wings and fly.

~Lindsay Hodges

Introduction

About *Words Alive*

Words Alive is a creative writing group for older people which began as a taster course offered by Engage With Age in Holywood Road Library, Belfast in 2009. Engage With Age were aware that older people have a rich store of experiences to draw on and that many are not able to get about easily and can feel isolated. So a course was offered to see if there was an interest in meeting and sharing thoughts and recollections, and writing down what might otherwise be lost – in their own words, their own voices, with their own take on life. They thought that it could be a way of meeting several inter-connected needs and interests in a creative way.

The initiative took off and *Words Alive* has continued to flourish as an inclusive group for first-time and seasoned writers from a wide range of backgrounds and with differing needs and abilities. The name of the group was coined by one of our founder members, Joan Lawlor. In 2012 we published a first anthology, *Pen to Paper*, which was well received and this encouraged us to arrange some readings of our work.

About *Words Alive Across Belfast*

Towards the end of 2013, Engage With Age suggested that we visit and read to residents in a couple of care homes. The response to these visits was so positive that *Words Alive* arranged to visit more care homes. Finding the response to be consistently enthusiastic, from staff and participants alike, the group undertook to make voluntary visits each month to various groups in community, church and day centres, sheltered dwellings and care homes.

This led to setting up an Outreach Project: *Words Alive Across Belfast*. For it had become clear, after visiting over 20 different venues, that very many of the people we read and chatted to on these outreach visits lacked the very stimulation that we ourselves were getting out of attending *Words Alive*. Let's face it, many of us elderly folk become invisible all too easily, with little to feed our creativity or sense of identity. This was our opportunity to defy that loss, in some small way.

About *Spreading Our Wings*

We came up with the idea of a second anthology that could be a resource, an aid to personal recollection. *Spreading Our Wings* contains poems and reflections that give a slice of lives lived. Each section focuses on a different topic, such as 'Early Days', 'Happiness and Heartache', or 'Popular Places and Pastimes'. At the end of each section there are some questions and suggestions to encourage people to talk about their own lives and opinions, to draw on their own treasure house of memories. It is our hope that, by bringing the book to groups and leaving it with them (and with any relevant staff member who can give support), the conversations may continue and not be confined only to our visits.

~John H Galbraith, Chair of Words Alive
~Ruth Carr, Facilitator

Table of Contents

THE RAG'N BONE MAN: Early Days

TALKING WITH GRAN: Family Snaps

MY FIRST DANCE: Popular Places and Pastimes

THAT FEARFUL NIGHT: Terrible Times

WITH LOVE: Happiness and Heartache

MORNING GLORY: The Natural World

ADJUSTING: Changing Times

BEFORE I KNEW: Reflections

FORGET ME NOT: Later Days

In memory of our fellow writer and friend, Marie Mathews

THE RAG'N BONE MAN
Early Days

THE RAG'N BONE MAN   Bernice Burrows

I heard the sound of horse's hooves on the cobble pavement and the yell "Rags, any auld rags". I leant over the back gate and saw a man with a horse and cart. He was going around the neighbourhood collecting old junk and rags. The horse was grey with a lovely, long mane of black hair and blinkers on its bridle. It looked huge.

That was in 1979. But now, the sound of horse's hooves strikes the cobble pavement outside my home and the same yell alerts me. For an instant, time stands still. The past meets the present.

I grab the first thing to hand, put it on and sling on a coat to run outside and find a horse and cart, with a man standing talking to one of my neighbours. Running down the street, I stop outside the neighbour's house.

"Are you the Rag'n Bone man?" I blurt out.

"He's right here," the neighbour replies, pointing to the man next to him.

It's like magic. I ask if I can stroke the horse and the man nods and smiles. Then I ask what he is doing on the streets of Belfast and if I can take a picture of him and his horse. Would the horse mind? He gives another reassuring nod, so I start clicking away on my mobile.

"That's proof that the Rag'n Bone man was here, in case people don't believe me."

"It's a dream, wake up!" he jokes, giving me a gentle shake.

Our laughter fills the air, and I listen to what he is saying to my neighbour who appears to be in his bare feet for some reason. It is a strange situation.

He explains that he is collecting furniture for charity and that he used to be in the trade a long while back. I see a twinkle in his eye as he tells me he is planning to make a return to the streets of Belfast.

"So you really are the Rag'n Bone man!"

"Oh he is," my neighbour adds, "look, he's took my socks!"

All three of us break into laughter.

When the conversation tails off, my neighbour goes inside and that leaves me and the Rag'n Bone man standing on the pavement. He takes up the horse's reins and I gently tap the horse to go on, then I wait until they are out of sight before I turn and walk back down the street. They disappear as quickly as they had appeared, as if by magic. But I have the photograph to prove they were here.

TRADESMEN FROM MY PAST   Denis Hyde

The coalman came on Mondays, often with a soot covered face. He tipped four bags of coal into our bunker.

Our pigman came early, he walked with a limp, collected the food waste we put out for his pigs.

I'd hear the paperboy whistling down the passage each day he delivered the 'telly'. When he called for the money he'd stop for a chat and a bit of craic.

Jack the milkman came before light, delivered the milk from his horse and cart. Mum put out bread and the horse came up our passage to get it.

LITTLE BIRD   Sue McCrory

It was a long time ago when I first drew breath at my grandmother's home. My birth weight was two pounds, four and a half ounces.

The midwife said, "Too small. Every day she will need twenty-four hour attention."

My grandmother quickly replied, "I'll look after her."

I had no nails, nor eye lashes, no hair and my skin was very dry. Every day my grandmother rubbed olive oil into my body, taking care not to remove any skin. She kept me alive by feeding me a small drop of milk through the filter of a fountain pen. Grandmother fed me this small portion of food several times daily.

She always kept me warm, she held me in her arms and had a special nursery chair that was just the right height to allow her to get up easily; we were a cosy pair. My grandmother held me close to her heart, our two heartbeats united in the enjoyment of the healthy warm glow that came from the welcoming open fire.

It was hard work for her looking after me twenty-four hours every day. I know it was a labour of love. Sometimes her arms would grow weary from holding me all the time. She called me her "Little Bird" and put me in a shoe box fitted out with a layer of cosy and warm cotton wool. Off I would go to sleep.

My grandmother did all this for me during the first six months of my life, without a break. She kept surrounding me with love and care, enabling me to soon become a healthy and contented baby.

THANK YOU GRANNY

THE URBAN COWBOY　　　　John H Galbraith

I was born in Newcastle Street in 1935.
Born into the dust of traffic teeming
the length of the Newtownards Road.

My lullaby was the sound of the fish man,
as he yelled from his horse-drawn cart:
"Fresh herrin's, Ardglass herrin's for sale."

I woke to the crash of steel-studded boots,
thousands of men tramping to the Shipyard,
shaking the heart of our East Belfast home.

My mother worked in the Ropeworks,
Dad worked in a factory, I never saw much of either –
they worked eight to six all week.

Every morning Mum left me at Gran's.
I was drawn to Grandad's shed out the back
to the window in the side wall.

My friends and I would stare in wonder –
a world of wood and steel on the bench,
a lathe and a drilling machine.

Files were laid out like soldiers; half rounds,
rough cut, rasps. Hammers and chisels on hooks.
We pretended they were our tools.

When we turned sixteen the pretence
became real: we signed up as apprentices.
Some in the Yard, some at Mackies, or the mill.

SKINKING

Gerry McCool

A chair was too high.
You had to kneel on it.
This restricted your natural movements.
Milk bottles were great.
They were the standard unit.
Just about half a saucepan
and twice a tumbler.
The basin took up too much room
in the sink for the fluid movement
of these important receptacles.
Twenty minutes of precise pouring
and careful measuring in
Granny's old Belfast sink.
Unknown to this day was the
ultimate purpose of this important work.
Archimedes may well have understood.
But we did not, for the same experiments
Would have to be repeated, tomorrow.

WASH DAY   John H Galbraith

Every time I smell Lifebuoy soap it's 1945 –
My Gran is bent over the Belfast sink
in the long corridor of her steam-filled kitchen.
Soap bubbles float about her head like a halo.
Her sleeves are rolled up to the elbows,
her arms look raw, plunged deep in hot water.
She rubs the red soap into Grandad's overalls
spread out on the glass-ribbed wash-board.
With hands like hammers up and down the board
she pummels the clothes, then throws them
into a bucket of clean, cold water.
I have a plunger to rinse them soap-free,
then out to the mangle. I turn the wheel
and the rollers spin, squeezing them almost dry
and Grandad's overalls are pegged on the line –
I can still see them now.

THE RAIN   Kate Glackin

It was pitch black outside.
Constant rain tapped my window,
the curtains shivered
and my bedroom door creaked.

I wasn't afraid.
I was six years old,
safe in my bed
and hugging my teddy bear.

I kissed him goodnight
and holding him tight
fell asleep.

JACK   Sue McCrory

When I was a schoolgirl our family had a dog called Jack. He had a beautiful black and white coat, large, kind eyes and sometimes we thought he smiled at us. On school mornings he would wait at our gate and walk with us. When we arrived he stayed put until we went in the school door and then he would turn for home. At three o'clock he would be waiting for us at the school gate to walk us home.

When I went to fetch a can of milk he accompanied me and sat at the door until I had poured four pints of milk into my can. I would also collect some cream from the crock where it was kept and off we would go with Jack leading the way back home. He was a clever, loyal dog with a very gentle manner.

Then came the sad time when he had to be put to sleep. We buried him in our orchard near his favourite spot. My sisters, brother and I collected wild flowers and made a posy to place on his grave each time we paid a visit.

We missed him for a very long time. I was broken-hearted.

GUM AND DOUGHNUTS   Sue McCrory

During WWII part of the American forces were based in a camp just outside Newcastle near my home. I was nine years old at the time and nosey. I got permission from my mother to go for a walk with my friend who was a few years older than me. We went along the footpath outside the base and there we met three American soldiers who attended the same church as us and whom my parents had met. One was called Tiny, he was over seven foot and was built like a tank.

The soldiers were kind to us and gave us presents: American red apples, chewing gum that was in long sticks and chicklets. They also gave us candy, coffee, biscuits, cake and doughnuts. Had we been older they would have given us nylon stockings, either with a seam or without. (If you got the ones without a seam, then you needed to take a black pen and draw the seam in yourself down the back of the stockings.) To others, the Americans gave beautiful hankies and rich fruit cake in the shape of a ring.

The day the soldiers left, the wife of one of the soldiers had her first baby, and by coincidence my married sister also had a baby on that day, 16th May, 1942.

FEELING THE CANE

Denis Hyde

When I did something wrong in the classroom, the teacher sent me to the headmaster's office to wait outside in a sweat, feeling tense and guilty.

The teacher rushed in to explain what happened. The Headmaster said, "O.K. let me deal with this."

He took his trusty cane from the cupboard, bent it, then he swished it and said, "I am going to punish you and I hope it will be the last time I have to do this."

He told me to hold out my hands as he examined them. I closed my eyes, held my breath and waited. Whoosh, whack the cane sang as he hit me. I opened my eyes after six of his best.

"Dismissed," he said. "Go and apologise."

SEEING SANTA ON CHRISTMAS EVE
Denis Hyde

Margaret who lived across the street was a good friend of my mum. She asked if she could take me into town to see Santa who was in the Co-op in York Street. Mum was delighted and told me to put on my duffle coat and school cap to keep me warm. I was excited and got ready in a flash.

We had to get two buses. They were damp and cold with the windows misted over. When we got into the shop it was all bustle and hustle, packed with Christmas shoppers who were pushing and shoving.

Margaret led me to the lift and it took us up to the second floor in no time at all. I was glad to get away from the shoppers on the ground floor.

When the lift doors opened, I began to regret our trip. Children were screaming, kicking and shouting that they wanted to see Santa. So did I, but I didn't want to get hurt and remained quiet and calm as we waited in the queue.

When it was my turn a giant of a man in a red Santa suit smiled at me, shook my hand and gave me a present. I could feel the outline of a board game. Margaret swiftly got me back in the lift. She was muttering something to herself about cheapskates as we made our way out of the store.

I thought we were going home but instead we walked through the town and into Robbs to meet another Santa.

This place wasn't so noisy. I was happy and tired, so after I had my photograph taken with another bearded man who gave me another present, which I was sure held another board game, all I wanted was to go home and hold onto my belief that there was a real Santa.

That night I was sure he existed and kept looking out my bedroom window to catch sight of the reindeer sleigh that would bring Santa to my chimney.

THE WATER BOARD MAN IN COOLFIN STREET
Myra Gibson

Let's go, for the Water Board man is coming
All the children into the street come running
To the man who showers water everywhere,
Take off your shoes and socks and abandon care.
As he turns the T-shaped rod into the ground
Out come cascades of water with gushing sound
Hurry, squish your feet in the cool, clear water
Splashing and splashing with delight and laughter.

Quick, see yourself on the beach at Crawfordsburn
For in a moment the T-shaped rod must turn,
Soon stopping the water coming from the mains.
You see the last drops escaping down the drains,
Now, go dry your feet, put on your socks and shoes,
Shout thanks to the Water Board man as he goes
Back to his office down in Donegall Square.
Leaving, in my mind, those times beyond compare.

THE BUDDING PHOTOGRAPHER   Denis Hyde

I took the coins I had saved in a jam-jar and put them in little brown bags to go to the corner shop where they were changed into crisp five pound notes. I was rich, for a boy of ten.

Mum and I went to town, to Woolworth's. I spied a camera which only cost fifty bob and came with a roll of black and white film. The frame you looked through to take a picture jutted out at the top of the camera. When we got home I took some photos of Mum and the neighbour's little girl.

I went to the chemist on the Cregagh Road to leave the film in to be developed. Having to wait for several days, my excitement mounted. I could hardly wait to see my first photographs.

But when I at last got them, they were a bit of a disappointment. I opened the folder to find that most of the heads and feet were cut off and some of the images were unrecognisable, more like the mystery objects for a quiz.

Never mind, I now know that you need practice to take perfect photos, in fact, you need practice to do most anything well.

THE STEAM TRAIN TO BANGOR Denis Hyde

On a Sunday morning my dad asks me if I would like to go to Bangor on the train. I say "Yes!" I take my pennies out of the piggy bank to play the slot machines.

We go on the bus from Castlereagh Road to Bridge End and walk slowly to Queen's Quay, then enter the station with excitement.

The smell of diesel hits my nose - thankfully it is a pleasant smell. I hear the whistle of a guard, but not for our train just yet. Dad gets our tickets and we wait a bit until the Bangor train comes in. I spot a machine in the corner which types out metal labels and I type out my name with it.

The train suddenly arrives out of nowhere, puffing black smoke that chokes me. We get a comfy seat on our own. The train shunts and rattles gently to and fro and off we go. We pass various places – Holywood, Helen's Bay, Crawfordsburn – we are nearly there…

In Bangor we walk down the hill on Main Street. There is no rain, it is a beautiful day but still a bit cold. I see people on the beach, lots of them swimming, they must be mad! I buy a 99 with a flake with my own money and go into Barry's Amusements. I can hear a man laughing as I go in the door with a handful of coins to play the fruit machines. I get fruit gums and a packet of sweets and I win some and lose some games.

Before we head back I go on the ghost train which is a bit scary but lots of fun. I am happy as happy can be. We catch the train about five and get home about 5.45pm, just in time for dinner.

THIS ARTEFACT   Gerry McCool

Your point is broken.
Is that why you were discarded?
Or did your bowman confront his hunting nemesis?
That majestic stag still bounds and springs escaping,
Or underground that disappearing bobtail.
Your shaft perhaps tangled in thick brambles,
Or in deep, dark, water, beyond reclamation.
A sense of loss, tempered by past successes.
A long trek with roughout tools in straw bags
From that bright chalk quarry, up on old Black Mountain
Down to the Lagan meadows of your homestead.
The time invested in the artistry of your finish:
Your bulb of percussion and rippling out striations.
Your three, long, fluted, pressure-pointed panels.
Not ever just an implement for hunting,
Your beauty apparent still, after four long millennia.

Over to You

- What are your childhood memories?
  Close your eyes: what can you see, ?
  What can you hear, taste, smell?

- Do you remember the Rag and Bone Man? Or other tradesmen who delivered to your door?
  What did they bring?

- Where did you grow up? What places do you remember going to?

- Were you taken to see Santa?
  When did you stop believing in Santa?

- Did you play at the sink? In the street?
  What were your favourite childhood games?

- Did you ever turn the handle of a mangle?
  Or help with household chores?

- Did you feel the cane?
  What did you get up to at school?

- Did you have any pets? What were they like?

- Tell us about your first camera, or first something else.

- Have you ever picked up an arrowhead or an old clay pipe and pondered about it like Gerry?

TALKING WITH GRAN
Family Snaps

TALKING WITH GRAN   John H Galbraith

Gran is that you sitting on my bed?
Are you here to listen or maybe
give me a scolding?
You cost me a lot of money,
I think all of the street was
at your funeral last month.
I'll need to get a loan
to pay for the wake.
Everyone wants a piece of you.
Maggie Clark wants your pots,
Rosie Brennan says you owe
her a tenner. I caught Lizzie Weir
searching your drawers.
She tried to steal that Easter photo.
You know, the one with the flowers
in your bonnet. Grandad and I walked
up the Castlereagh hills for them.
Your great grand-daughter is getting
so like you. She's into everything –
no wonder we called her Chrissie.
Yes, I know Percy Sledge just died.
And yes, "Every man needs a woman."

Couldn't sleep last night, thinking about
you. Getting near your birthday.
I'll get you some flowers.
Got to go Gran, God bless. Love you.

GRANDAD'S SHED   John H Galbraith

The shed isn't used much now he's gone.
Gran says she won't go in anymore.
But it needs cleared out, and it's my job to do it.
Better I take what I want, let the rest
go elsewhere. There are all sorts of files inside:
rough cut, flats, cross-cut, rasps, all set out on hooks.
There's a grinder growing a mountain of dust
beneath it. Perched in a corner his
hammers, alongside a power saw and drill
machine, poking out from a canvas sheet.
The drawers gape like open mouths holding
boxes of screws and nails marked
by size and type. At the back of one,
two pieces of unfinished marquetry,
the craft blades carefully wrapped in oil-soaked rags.
These are the lifetime tools of my Grandad,
I feel him in every dust mote in this shed.

EXTRA CURRICULUM   Diane Weiner

"There's two in that."

"No. there's only one."

"There's definitely two!"

Thus went the conversation between my sister and me as we dived into huge sacks of odd stockings. Our task was to pair them as best we could. Two ladders sold for sixpence and one ladder for a shilling. We were both still at school but homework or no homework we had to start pairing the stockings after school for the next day when my father would sell them at St George's Market.

My mother tackled the Blaxnit Cushion Sole Socks. Bales of them, all odd. Again these had to be paired as close as possible. Women went crazy for them. It was the fifties, money was scarce and a great bargain was to be had.

My father also sold neckless jumpers, again manufactured by a local company. To this day I don't know why the necklines were never finished, just stitched up slits where the opening should have been. Again these were snatched up by customers who were prepared to finish the garments themselves. My father also sold silk ties and linen tablecloths and sheets.

I often wondered what my friends from the posh school I attended would think if they could see how I spent my evenings. At times when I helped my father at different markets I was always on the lookout for my school uniform. If I saw one approaching I would hide under the stall.

We gain education from many sources and situations in life. My sister and I learnt that we had to work to survive as a family and as people. I am forever grateful for that and hope that by example we have passed on that ethic to the younger members of our family.

MEMORIES FROM AN OLD PHOTO

John H Galbraith

In this photograph from nineteen thirty-nine
you can see Mum and Dad. He looks so swell,
another David Niven or Errol Flynn.
He's wearing his silken waistcoat, wrapped
round his chest like body armour.
Baggy trousers, two tone shoes, black tie
complete his mourning dress for that hard day.
My mum stands by his side. She looks sad,
perhaps the sun's too bright for her weak eyes,
or has she been been crying for her son?
My father has put on a face of stone,
he wears it often, since my brother's gone.
So many years passed until my father died.
In all that time he kept his stony face.

A MEMENTO   **Bernice Burrows**

Treasured by me but no use to another -
this photograph, taken when I was five,
in school, my teacher putting my hair in pigtails.
An old photo, given to me by my father
who'd kept it in his jacket pocket - a memento of
the child taken away from him, too early?
A child he would meet as a woman,
giving her a fragment of memory, faded like
the photograph – two memories, merging into one.

THE RATHER LARGE GENTLEMAN

Sue McCrory

Seventy-five years ago during the War my father had a black Austin Seven car. At that time all cars in Northern Ireland were subject to wartime regulations, one of which was that headlights had to be fitted with shutters to reduce the light from them. There were restrictions on the amount of petrol that could be sold to each owner and this was controlled by the issue of petrol stamps. My father was in business and was allowed extra in order to keep his car on the road and make deliveries.

I remember one time my sister and I were in the car with my father driving when we approached a steep hill. He stopped to give a rather portly gentleman a lift. We moved into the front passenger seat so that the man could place his two massive bags in the back and then arrange himself beside them.

Our little car struggled to get up the hill under all that weight. It was on the verge of engine failure every few yards until, with a chug-chug, it gave up the ghost. Father asked everyone to get out and unload the bags. He decided that it would be easier on our car if we walked up the hill.

We started walking and helped the man with his luggage. We could hear the little Austin stuttering all the way up the hill. By the time we arrived at the top there it sat right as rain while we puffed and panted. Father whispered to us that the car had been carrying too much weight to get up the hill.

Fortunately there were no more hills between us and home, and in half an hour, we arrived there safely, having delivered the portly gentleman and his bags to his destination on the way. That was the kind of thing my father used the wee Austin for back then.

MODEL 1974   Diane Weiner

You left so suddenly, it was nearly a year before we could move your car from the front of the house.

I think we felt that a part of you was still with us while we could look out the window and see it, just where you always left it.

Now it sits in the garage and has done for all these years.

I remember the look of pride and joy on your face the day you brought it home. My mother was speechless, she thought it such an extravagance!

Now, when I slip into those big leather seats, I lose myself in memories. Your Atkinson silk tie, which you so often removed, sits neatly folded in the glove compartment, beside it the owner's manual and the service record booklet – although hardly touched they have yellowed with age.

In a side pocket some Green Shield stamps, never redeemed and a tin of boiled sweets unopened, long past their sell-by date.

The tax disc is still on display, JAN 1971, with the fee of £25.00 stamped on it.

The mascot which once stood proudly on the bonnet, now sits on the passenger seat, carefully wrapped in cotton to protect it.

I knocked it off its perch the first time I drove your car. I hit the gate post, couldn't handle the power steering which was relatively new in those days.

I never drive it now, but I am its keeper, so I shall continue to reminisce from time to time and lose myself in memories.

OUR OBSERVER

Gerry McCool

The mirror hung in our kitchen,
A wedding present in 1948,
Oversaw the family, one by one.
I combed my hair, checked my tie
Before leaving for school or church,
My mother used a puffer and a brush,
My father fingered Brylcreem from a jar,
His black hair combed in wavy lines
Like a piece of liquorice from that time.
He often shaved at that old mirror too,
Not in the bathroom – we had no bathroom.

Forty years later he still used that mirror
In a newer home now but still in the kitchen.
Not the shape or style now for the bathroom,
The mirror still watched over everyone,
With all the familiarity of a religious icon.
I grew up with long hair, then a beard,
My brother too resembled a long-haired hippy.
When my son was four one day
We passed a religious shop
He said 'Dad, why is that shop full
Of pictures of you and Uncle Jim?'

I looked in the mirror the morning I was married;
My hair was shorter, neater, in my strangled suit
I spoke into the old mirror and asked
'Oh God, is this what it's all come to?'

A TRUE STORY   Myra Gibson

In a cabinet, in a palace, lies a gift of linen from Ulster, for a wedding.

My brother brought home cloth pieces from his workplace: "They are too grand to use as rags," he said.

My Aunt selected a large square of the cloth and hemmed round its edges on her Singer sewing machine. She gave me this now beautiful white linen damask supper cloth.

In my special box it rests, a keepsake of my caring Aunt and her sewing craft. She's gone now, along with the skills of the Ulster weavers who spun the cloth in 1960 for a Princess.

THE BOY WHO MADE A METEORITE

Gerry McCool

We were through playing marbles,
I had just lost twelve – eleven.
Two hours after school but this boy was not tired yet.
It was time for some play-dough engineering:
Space was the theme but I'd only blue and yellow,
I would make Earth and he would make the rocket leaving.
Yellow continents were pressed into a bluish globe.
I sneaked a look to check the rocket's progress.
Alas, no rocket, just a purple ball…
Ah, a planet. Is that the moon then?
No Grandad, that's the meteorite
That's going to crash into Earth and kill the dinosaurs.
Oh, I looked around to see who might be prompting.
No, this four year old was aeons ahead of me,
Drawing a boat was my P1 best effort.
We never got as far as meteorites, triceratops, or mass extinctions.

MY GRAND-DAUGHTER'S FIRST OP

Sue McCrory

In the course of a telephone conversation with my daughter-in-law Chris, I enquired: "And how is Charlotte doing?"

Chris replied, "Good and busy. She had her first surgery and the operation was a success."

"That's gratifying," I replied. "And who was the patient?"

The line was poor and I couldn't make out what she said. I repeated the question more loudly, still unclear. "Who?"

"A cow," Chris bellowed.

GRANNIE   John H Galbraith

I remember before her passing
I felt the darkness coming since the summer.
It was like sitting in the sunshine
then the sky clouds over, and everything darkens.
I remember before her passing.
How she would laugh with me , then pause,
as if waiting for the storm clouds to pass.
Then she would look at me to speak again.
I remember before her passing.
Suddenly at the end she was not old,
all her worries and pain in her face
dissolved into a teenager once again.

THE PHONE THAT NEVER RINGS

Diane Weiner

It sits by your bedside,
where it always sat,
disconnected and silent.
It never rings and it never will.
Messages of love spoken long ago,
recorded within.
Someday
Someday I will listen.
Until then, poignant words and memories
Will stay, locked inside the phone that never rings.

THE LAST TIME I SAW GRANDMA TINI

John H Galbraith

I remember her
beside a blazing winter fire;
stirring the porridge pot with a wooden spoon.
A grand old Scottish lady from the shipyards of Govan.
Grandpa died that summer, he was eighty-four.
She said it wouldn't be long before
she lay beside her beloved Archie.
I was unable to travel when she died,
unable to say goodbye
to my beloved Grandma Tini.

BOY   Diane Weiner

My dog is a handsome little fellow. He had a prime position at my window but a new dining table and four chairs necessitated his move. He now sits in the middle of the table. I don't know where or when he was made but I do know where he came from and he is priceless to me.

My father purchased an old leather shop many years ago and being the wheeler-dealer that he was, he asked the seller to throw in the contents as a luck penny and quite a luck penny it proved to be. He sold webs of leather, heels and soles to repair shoes, hundreds of laces, and all the machinery to Rogans, a large shoe repair shop based on the Shankill Road. An old lady had lived and died above the shop and it was among her possessions that the dog was found.

My mother took an immediate shine to him, and installed him at her window where he sat until this week. She called him "Boy" and had many conversations with him, albeit one-sided.

As I look at him now my heart is filled with mixed emotions, joy for the memories of happy times my family shared, sadness for the loss of loved ones and gladness that instead of looking out at the world Boy's gaze is now fixed firmly on me.

IN LOVING MEMORY   Kate Glackin

Frank's family were devastated. He was a kind and loving, gentle giant. His days were now numbered after months of suffering and medication. There was no hope of survival. He lay still on his bed, eyes closed, body quiet and unconscious.

Prayers and tears poured out as they kept vigil by his bed with great compassion. In the silent hours candles were lit and the prayers continued.

Suddenly, as dawn was breaking, his body twitched and his eyes opened. Slowly he sat up in the bed. He looked to the right hand side of the room and a beautiful smile appeared on his pale face. His arms were outstretched and he leaned forward as if to embrace an unexpected loved one. He called out, loud and long: "Aaah! Aaah!"

He then fell back gently on the bed, eyes closed, still smiling peacefully with his arms folded across his chest. The family huddled together in shock and bewilderment (because, however imminent death is, we are never quite prepared). They quietly formed a circle around him.

This is a true story. I was there. Frank was my Dad.

Over to You

- What would you say to your gran, or another loved one?

  Try writing a letter: Dear…

  Do you have fond memories of other family members?

- Pick a photograph and tell its story, either as you remember it, or make it up!

- Do you have something that was passed down to you?

  Something that reminds you of other times, or the person it belonged to?

- Do you have grandchildren, nieces, nephews?

  What do they get up to?

  What would you like to tell them about your life?

MY FIRST DANCE
Popular Places and Pastimes

MY FIRST DANCE   Diane Weiner

I knew my dress was beautiful – it was C&A's finest. It was made from cotton seersucker with a tiered skirt and in my favourite colour – lilac. My aunt made the petticoat, yards upon yards of tulle which had been soaked in starch to make it stiff so that the dress would sit out. Some of my friends were lucky, their relatives had sent them dresses from America, these were really spectacular.

My taste in music changed dramatically in 1958. From singing "On top of old Smokey", "Now is the hour", "How much is that doggie in the window?", I now joined in with Tommy Steele "Singing the Blues" and jived to Elvis and his "Blue Suede Shoes." My friends had taught me how to jive and now I hoped to learn the waltz, and the quickstep at Sammy Leckey's dance classes.

I set off on the 33 bus. It stopped at the City Hall, convenient to where I was to meet my friends. Sitting on the top deck, as usual, I was very careful to hold my dress close as I climbed the stairs – very ladylike. I got off the bus and as I passed the front of the City Hall I felt a tap on my shoulder. I looked around and a very kind lady said, "Love, your petticoat has been trailing behind you since you got off the bus."

I was mortified. I reeled it in and bunched it up as best I could. Aunt Lily wasn't such a good stitcher after all.

Somehow I made it to the Y.M.C.A and reached my friends. A quick repair was made in the Ladies. I can't remember where the pins came from but we managed to secure the petticoat and I made it to the dance... and so my dancing days began.

Things didn't always go smoothly. I found it difficult to find a partner tall enough and sometimes I was a wallflower. Girls didn't dance with each other in those days and boys did not dance with girls taller than themselves. However, a whole new world opened up for me: my first kiss, first embrace, heartache and happiness in equal measure.

I wouldn't have missed those days for the world.

DANCE NIGHT WITH SALLY   Diane Weiner

The small dance hall was above a few shops at the bottom of the Woodstock Road, it only opened on Saturday night. The music came from a little turn-table which was operated by an elderly gentleman decked out in his funeral suit.

The first night I went, Sally arrived at my door and I couldn't believe my eyes. She had rollers in her hair, slippers on her feet, wearing not a trace of make-up. I was wearing my C&A's best, with pumps on my feet and a smear of lipstick, the only make-up I was allowed.

She must have seen the surprised look on my face because before I could say anything she put her finger to her lips to shush me and pointed to a paper bag she was carrying. Then it dawned on me. Her parents were very strict and probably didn't know she was going dancing.

As soon as we arrived at the dance she headed for the toilets with me in tow. Immediately the transformation began. On went the make-up, off came the rollers and when she removed her coat she was wearing a very pretty dress. Last thing out of the bag was a pair of very fetching stiletto heels in brilliant white. She looked a million dollars.

Sally probably got rushed that night, she usually did. I was probably a wallflower, I usually was. She was eighteen and I was fifteen. Some memories just stay with you forever.

SINATRA SINGS   John H Galbraith

FRANK SINATRA, THE VOICE SINGS, CLOSE TO YOU.

I BELIEVE, I COULD HAVE DANCED ALL NIGHT.

'SWONDERFUL, I GET A KICK OUT OF YOU.

YOUNG AT HEART, IN THE STILL OF THE NIGHT.

WITCHCRAFT, I'VE GOT A CRUSH ON YOU.

I'VE GOT YOU UNDER MY SKIN, NIGHT AND DAY.

I'M IN THE MOOD FOR LOVE, EMBRACABLE YOU.

TIME AFTER TIME, THE GIRL THAT GOT AWAY.

YOU MAKE ME FEEL SO YOUNG, AS TIME GOES BY.

TAKING A CHANCE ON LOVE, COUNT ON ME.

OLD BLACK MAGIC, WHAT KIND OF FOOL AM I.

MY FUNNY VALENTINE, COME FLY WITH ME.

IN THE WEE SMALL HOURS, SHE'S FUNNY THAT WAY.

OLD BLUE EYES, HAD A VERY GOOD YEAR, HIS WAY.

THE JIVER   John H Galbraith

Tonight he is wearing his best dancing shoes:
blue leather uppers, polished like mirrors,
and two-inch thick crepe soles that squeak
each time he bounces on the Plaza ballroom floor.
The bottom of his Teddy boy coat swings
around his knees, its velvet collar white
with dandruff, the black shirt is sweat-soaked
as he rocks to the music of the Kirchen band.
A red slim-jim tie sways around his neck,
drainpipe trousers are plastered to thin calves
his Tony Curtis hairstyle, is slathered
in Brylcreem, the curl falls over his forehead.
The lights dim, suspended from the ceiling
the crystal ball casts light on the dancers
the rotating bandstand brings Ted Heath
and his band blasting out an Elvis song.
The jiver pumps his long legs, arms swing,
the ballroom floor bounces to his beat,
the dancers give him and his lady
the centre of the floor, rocking and rolling
fit to jive to the very last hour.
The Plaza is living its Friday night promise.

MY FIRST RECORD PLAYER   Denis Hyde

When my Uncle Jim died in 1962, in Mount Street, my mum and aunt went to clear out his house. One of the things they brought home, was a portable record player, a Dansette, which they gave to me in memory of him.

There was also a number of 78 records but they were a bit scratchy, and were not really my type of music. Then my dad's workmate from the Co-op in Templemore Avenue gave me a load of 45rpm records which played brilliantly.

My favourites were:

"Ticket to Ride" - The Beatles

"Island of Dreams" - The Springfields

"I Remember You" - Frank Ifield

"Heartache by the Number" - Guy Mitchell

"I Love You Because" - Jim Reeves

I mostly played these when Mum and Dad were out, because when she was home she used to shout "Turn that down please, I can't hear myself think!"

SATURDAY MATINEES   John H Galbraith

Where are you now, my Saturday morning heroes?
Where are you now, Tom Mix and Hopalong Cassidy?
John Wayne and Gabby Hayes have left the screen,
The Lone Ranger no longer shouts Hi Ho Silver
and Tonto doesn't hide behind a pile of rocks.
The echoes of six shooters have passed from the Popular.
The New Princess entry is sealed with garbage,
the Classic Picture House and the Royal Cinema
have become The British Home Stores and Starbucks.
Sunday opening for the troops at the Imperial is ended,
Corky cannot get any money from the cinema queues.
Gone are the naive days of the forties
destroyed by the builders' wrecking ball.

HELENS BAY 1950   John H Galbraith

Not far away, there is the green of farmland,
in the distance a brown lane drives through it.
There is the smell of cooking from a nearby farm,
cows wander among the fields near the beach,
a fence keeps them from walking into the sea.
I take off my shoes and socks, gritty sand divides
my toes as I walk slowly towards the sun-bathers.
Close by, the muscle-men put on a show.
They pose for the delight of young women.
Someone has brought a set of weights,
a young man with shoulders like a brick wall
huffs and puffs performing Olympic lifts.
Raindrops fall softly, then increase rapidly.
Within minutes all that is on the beach
is a set of weights and a few muscle-men,
their feet glued into the soft wet sand.

HAND WALLOPING AT DUNDROD

Gerry McCool

Heading out past Tornaroy
up onto the Flowbog Road
Two miles yet to the big river
up there at Dundrod
Four boys, each fourteen,
on a hot summer's day in June
Escaping city confines
for the mountains, on their own.

No rods allowed, nor reels,
no nets, nor floats nor line,
Hands only, the single rule
and our take home limit five.

We turned there at the Hairpin Bend,
from the bridge I looked below
Into a little, culverted stream
which went underneath the road.
Just six feet wide, six inches deep,
but oh what there was in that burn –
A beautiful dinky, rainbow trout
with scarcely room to turn.

No point in catching the lovely fish
we were still on our way out.
So, let him stay fresh on this warm day
he'd be there if we'd a Dundrod drought.

So, we built up a weir of rocks and stones
and left him there in the water.
Headed on up to the big river, then
expecting hand-walloping slaughter.
Now we'd heard old hands calling it 'tickling' trout
but I've never seen one caught that way
When you touch one, there's a silver flash
then its forty fast yards away.

You've got to watch and wait, and splash a finger
and guide him to his rock
Where he will shelter in security
until you grab him in a lock.

He comes out in one deft movement
and is tossed up on the bank
Before he's a chance to wriggle free
He's one more in your tank.
On that day out at Dundrod river
we pulled out forty nine.
Put back forty-four again
and kept to our quota of five.

But I looked forward to our bonus
back down beside the old school
Ah but when we finally got the length
He'd absconded from his pool.

I blinked and stared in disbelief
Til a wee man shouted over
'Ha if it's your dinner that you're looking for,
he was taken by Archie the otter.'
So, a warning to you young fishermen,
whatever you try to claim,
You are not the only contender here,
There's other players at this game!

FRIDAY FISH MARKET   Denis Hyde

I open the glass door to the stalls,
the smell of fish hits my nose,
strong as the Ardglass boat loaded with herring.

I see the beady eyes of a lobster staring at me
begging to be free. It's too late - bought
by a Chinese couple – destined for the pot.

And there the white paper bags of dulse,
Mum's favourite, often spread on bread and butter
to make the perfect sarni.

The man comes over, his mouth
opens and closes like a fish.
"What can I do for you?"

"I want some haddock."
Two pieces for three pounds.
Not bad. That's dinner sorted.

A TRICK OF THE LIGHT   John H Galbraith

The dog head of his walking stick
sits snug within his right palm;
the knuckles skinned and bruised,
finger tips yellowed from smoking
his matchstick roll-ups.
His other hand pulls open the door
and he struggles into the street.
One foot at a time his three legs propel him
over the cracks in the pavement.
Watery sunshine spills through the clouds
reflects on his bifocals.
Beating the pain to get to the bookies,
he fingers the docket –
a fiver on the winner, even money.
And in that slant of sun, he feels lucky.

SIXTY-FIVE YEARS AGO   Sue McCrory

I was taking a stroll with my friend round the Royal County Down Golf Club. The sun felt very warm and the grass looked even greener than usual. The mountains were so blue. Everyone had a smile on his or her face. What a difference good weather makes.

My friend suddenly halted and said in a stage whisper,

"Sue, do you know who that is on your left? It's King Leopold of Belgium."

It was the era of the fifties and people loved to collect autographs. I had no pen or paper. I looked around the grass and spotted a discarded Woodbine cigarette packet.

I borrowed a pen and asked the King for his autograph. Without batting an eyelid he graciously took the cigarette packet and signed it with a flourish.

FORTY-SEVEN TRIPS   Gerry McCool

I was still just fourteen in May '66,
Two nights in a sleeping bag outside the old Ritz.
Watched over and frowned on by the Fisherwick clock,
A few sins were committed to see this guy go rock.

Fifty years on, and this time it's Rome
To see someone special, with someone special from home
Our paths will converge here, as in Berlin and Toulouse,
To visit new places – hey, what an excuse.

Beckoned, drawn back, to the Baths of Caracalla
More used to the high notes of La Traviata.
On stage, squeezed between Vivaldi and Bizet,
The old jester from Duluth, can make it all seem so easy.

'Never-ending' is this tour, it keeps keeping on,
Could this be the last year? The itinerary's so long.
No chance with this guy, he's not knockin' on heaven
So, prepare and get ready for trip forty-seven!

ROCKET TO THE MOON   Gerry McCool

Smooth, continuously curved,

Inverted plum-bob.

A doorless doorway, a panoramic porthole.

Room for three inside, cozy together.

Red and white checked border,

Reminiscent of Hergé.

Far more mileage than the space shuttle,

A pound per trip, a reasonable price

To open up young minds

Boosted by these early lift-offs.

NASA would be so pleased.

WORLD HOPPING   Marjorie Jardine

Let's hop on a ferry and go on high
Just leave all your troubles and call at Shanghai
We'll swing into Tokyo then reach for the sky
With champagne on ice in a plane bound for Dubai
With magic on hold we'll end up with a blast
With a promise to keep the best wine to the last.

ON THE BENCH   Gerry McCool

A twenty minute walk from my own place. The great open spaces of Lady Dixon Park. A mahogany bench recessed in a lovely hawthorn hedge, sheltered from the breeze, and facing the afternoon sun. An overflow section of rose beds, busy at the annual show in July, secluded through the remainder of the year.

I would rather carry a book down there, and read it in peace and solitude, oblivious to time, the world, and even cell phones, than read it at home, where the nearby normality can often intrude or even overwhelm.

On the bike, I can use it as a first staging post on the way to the equally tranquil Lagan Tow Path – or the reverse on the way back when I need a bit of a rest before the last uphill stretch home again! I have spent many a happy hour there, with bits of picnics, or a cool drink, and a good book.

I am not the first though to discover the enjoyment of this spot. Another man found it long before I did and he liked it so much his family graciously sponsored the bench and its upkeep. The legend on the plaque reads:

Mr Charles Dudley 1917-1983.

It was his favourite place in all the world.

What a great judge!

Over to You

- Did <u>you</u> put on your dancing shoes?
At Betty Staff's, Sammy Leckey's, or The Plaza?
What other places were there?
What was your best memory?
And your worst?

- What was your local Picture House?
How many can you name? Any special memories?
What were your favourite films?

- Was there a particular place you liked to frequent?
What was it like? What did you get up to?
Where do you like to go now?

- Is there somewhere you like to sit now, a bench, a café, a window with a particular view?

- Do you remember your first record player, or guitar, or skates, or high heels, or Doc Martens, or your first car, or some other first precious thing?
Tell us about it.

- If the sky's the limit, what would you really like to do, or have a go at?

- Would you like to be a youngster today?

THAT FEARFUL NIGHT
Terrible Times

THAT FEARFUL NIGHT   John H Galbraith

after 'Do Not Go Gentle Into That Good Night' by Dylan Thomas

I shall not go easy into that fearful night
Now that I am old I shall fight all the way.
I have seen the dying of the light.

My age does not bring wisdom or make me right
Wise men have seldom shown us the way.
I shall not go easy into that fearful night.

Religious people preach and take delight
In telling sinners to get on their knees and pray.
I have seen the dying of the light.

Politicians look down from Stormont's height,
Tell us to pay the taxes and avoid the darkening day.
I shall not go easy into that fearful night.

Generals say that war will save us from plight
But all these wise people cannot stop the fight.
I have seen the dying of the light.

Peace and forgiveness is wanted in the twilight
Give me a handshake and we will keep hate at bay.
I shall not go easy into that fearful night.
I have seen the dying of the light.

THE SOMME, JULY 1916   Myra Gibson

They marched down the road together,
Smiling comrades all together,
Waving goodbye all together,
To family and friends together.

In trenches they fought together,
Unsmiling faces all together,
Died where they fell all together,
Brothers and friends together.

Bodies lost in mud together,
Never to come home all together,
Names chiselled in stone all together,
Comrades together, forever.

A SURVIVOR OF THE GREAT WAR LAMENTS FOR HIS LOST COMRADE   Myra Gibson

Quick, send them over the top, they said.
Now they're a heap of glorious dead.
Six months will see it over, they said.
Four years gone, millions of sons lie dead.

I've been to no-man's land to find my friend,
I've passed the dead and dying on the way,
I've missed the bullets that the enemy sends,
I could not find him in that bloody fray.

Quick, send them over the top, they said.
Now they're a heap of glorious dead.
Six months will see it over, they said.
Four years gone, millions of sons lie dead.

BOMBS ON BELFAST   John H Galbraith

Death paid a visit to Belfast at Easter
in nineteen forty-one. We didn't know
our lives were about to change.
I only knew that the big barrage balloons
were inching up into the evening sky
and I wanted one, just as much as I
wanted to be a sailor like my uncle.
But they don't allow six year old boys
into the Royal Navy.
Mum put me to bed early, then she pulled
me out of it in the middle of the night.
The air-raid sirens were screaming
like pigs being slaughtered. People were running
in the street, I heard bangs coming from the
Shipyard and someone was yelling for everyone
to stay indoors. We got under the stairs but the
house shook. Dad dug us out and we stood
in the street. I was cold, wet and scared.
There were very few searchlights and they
did not appear to concern the Nazi planes.
Our Ack-Ack guns were popping at them,
we could see they were not doing any damage
to the planes that were like ships in the sky.

Bombs fell like confetti, fire was eating
East Belfast, the Shipyard and Ropeworks.
We started to walk to the Castlereagh hills
Seeing everything we loved being destroyed.

ANNIVERSARY   John H Galbraith

I remember that night in April,
Mum said the Nazis had forgotten us.
And if the bombers came we had
the barrage balloons and Ack-Ack.
The bombers came on Easter Tuesday.
Bombs fell everywhere on Belfast;
Shipyard, the Ropeworks, churches,
aircraft factory, shops and homes.
Granda said they wouldn't be back.
He was wrong. On the fourth night of May
mum pulled me out of bed to see the stars,
I watched the clouds shred slowly,
it seemed thousands of fairy lights
were flying past in the cold night air.
Then the bombers let go their loads.
Incendiary bombs came down like confetti,
Land mines fell on the shipyard,
The Newtownards Road was destroyed.
We never got back into our house,
Most of it was lying in Newcastle Street.

1941   John H Galbraith

When East Belfast became a wasteland;
when incendiary bombs fell like blazing rain;
when my home became a furnace, then a ruin
where Newcastle Street once stood:
where cemetery bones lay scattered;

where firemen from Dublin fought the flames
that consumed a country that wasn't theirs.
Perhaps today their actions offer hope.

CITY AT WAR John H Galbraith

We ripped away the large pieces of debris,
they were taken to the rear by bulldozers,
Our eyes were constantly searching for movement
in the rubble. Carefully the smaller masonry
was removed by hand and transferred
by human chain. We had been digging
out the dead and the maimed all day.
Dust filled the air, our eyes full of tears,
we were exhausted. The rescue dogs lay
too tired to move, their large eyes alert,
showing willingness to keep on searching.
Eventually darkness stopped us digging,
other teams continued under floodlight,
we knew there was little hope of life.
But there was always a chance of a survivor.

BLACK FRIDAY, 1972　　　　　Denis Hyde

Mum and I were going home from Portstewart on an Ulsterbus Express to Belfast. When it came to Royal Avenue, the bus driver said, "You have to get off the bus as soon as you can." This was because of all the bombs that were going off. We could hear so many explosions going off in the background.

We were rushing with two suitcases along Royal Avenue when another blast went off and we could see black smoke. It was rising from Oxford Steet bus station.

"How will we get home, the roads are choc-a-bloc in the city centre," pondered Mum.

We decided to hail a black taxi even though we were both nervous as kittens. Some roads were blocked but we got home at last.

I will never forget that day in Belfast in 1972.

THE DAY I CLEARED SMITHFIELD

Diane Weiner

One Sunday morning in May 1972 when the "Troubles" were rife, I decided to clear a mound of papers which were accumulating in my roof space. Some of them were personal, others business, there were enough to fill a large bin bag. I decided to take them to my business the next morning as the bin-men collected on a Monday.

I left home early and arrived at Gresham Street before the shop had opened. As I had to go to the Passport Office I left the bag outside where it could be seen. Off I went, did my business and nonchalantly made my way back an hour later.

As I approached the area I realised there was a bomb scare. Smithfield Market and the surrounding streets had been evacuated. I could see a crowd of people, including my family, gathered at Upper North Street. Making my way over to them I was horrified to be told that my bin-bag had been blown up by the bomb-squad and my papers had been floating about the area for all and sundry to see who the culprit was. IT WAS ME!

Those shopkeepers were baying for my blood and who could blame them. The police were also on the scene. Only my poor father's pleading stopped them from charging me with placing an unidentified object in a public place, causing the evacuation of a large area and wasting police time.

It took some time to live that one down but eventually my neighbours forgave me. Probably relieved that on this occasion it wasn't actually a bomb.

Little did we know that what was to follow would devastate us all and change some lives forever.

DIARY ENTRY, JANUARY 1974   Diane Weiner

Sat 9th: Shop blown asunder
          "Happy New Year!"

Sun 10th: Held up at home
          By a man with a gun
          Left with a legacy
          No pills can dispel
          Forever reliving
          My weekend from Hell.

HOMELESS   **Bernice Burrows**

I am homeless, no less a person
than you who have a roof over your head
and food in your stomach.
I struggle day by day wondering where
my next meal will come from.
I do not have a choice,
I am not a "Beggar", or a "Tramp"
Simply homeless.
Just look at me, what do you see?
I am homeless, no less a person.

CAN I HELP YOU?   Kate Glackin

It was a foggy, wet, Monday morning. I was sipping coffee and looking out of my side kitchen window when I noticed three young men in dark anoraks with black woollen hats pulled down over their ears. They were sauntering up next door's long path and whispering to each other. My neighbour and his wife were away. These lads were acting suspiciously. I ran to my front door and noticed from there that one of them had disappeared. I felt I had to do something, so I shouted loudly, "Can I help you?"

They replied that they had come to fix my neighbour's guttering. This seemed unlikely, there were no tools or materials in sight. I knew they were up to no good and felt wary of them. Suddenly the one who had disappeared came running out from the side of the garage and dropped something metallic. They all darted down the path and into a side road. I was in a state of shock and phoned the police.

Three constables arrived within twenty minutes.

The piece of metal dropped was a broken padlock. Apparently one lad had climbed over the small garage roof and broken the padlock to gain entry to the rear of the house. I was interviewed and gave a statement. The constables congratulated me on my alertness and the efficient way I had handled the situation. I smiled, still feeling a bit dazed by the experience.

My neighbours arrived home fairly swiftly and repaired the back door. They also fitted a new padlock. Their house was equipped with all the required safety devices to deter a burglar during the dark hours, but no one would suspect a break-in attempt in broad daylight. In fact, the police since informed me that most break-ins occur in broad daylight.

My neighbours thanked me generously. To them it was clear that my question to the intruders – "Can I help you?" saved their house from being robbed. I was just delighted that I had been looking out my window when they came sauntering up the path.

A DAY AT CANCER OUTPATIENTS

John H Galbraith

Sally the technician calls Jessie's name,
she struggles to get up from her chair.
Her daughters bend over her, lift the
six stone lady with care, and help her to her feet.
She smiles at her girls, and tells everyone
she will see us later, we give her words of love.
My neighbour shuffles in her seat,
pretends to straighten her turban
and wipes away a tear.
Our ranks dwindle each day,
we slump in our chairs and wait.
Soon it will be our turn for the machine.
Radiotherapy brings nausea and pain
but it also provides a bubble land of hope.

Over to You

- Did you have any relatives in the First or Second World Wars?
  Do you know what happened to them?

- The Blitz affected lots of parts of Belfast.
  Do you have any family stories about that time?

- Have you ever cleared Smithfield?
  Or nearly died of embarrassment?

- In times of war, conflict and illness people often show great courage and resilience, laughter as well as tears. Do you have any memories of hard times that show the light side in spite of the dark?

WITH LOVE
Happiness and Heartache

WITH LOVE

Denis Hyde

Brick by brick
Cement it with love.
Wood to floor
Fit it with love.
Plaster to wall
Smooth it with love.
Stroke by stroke
Paint it with love.
Clean the room well
Leave it with love.
Let the room out
To a couple in love.

DRIFTWOOD   John H Galbraith

That Summer afternoon
lying in a sand dune in Scotland.
You lay beside me, the wind in your hair,
we held each other and planned our future.
The sea beat a lonely song on the beach,
I picked up a piece of driftwood.
And carved our names,
I still have it.

AGE OF AQUARIUS   Gerry McCool

I came at last to the special place.
I had been seeking to return there for some time.
It had been forty seven years since I went there
on my first true voyage of exploration and discovery.
The fifty foot cliff that I remembered was actually
more like twelve feet high. Strangely, just four miles
from the city centre, not yet torn up or redeveloped,
if anything the little mountain copse was even more
remote and virtually inaccessible.

The last time I tried to find it I ran out of daylight,
my only achievement being an atmospheric picture
of a wispy, mysterious moon floating just above the
horizon, and then when I got home I heard on the
ten o'clock news that Neil Armstrong had died that day.

I still remember your green and black banded mini
dress, your long dark hair, and your false eye-lashes
which presented a constant look of mild surprise.
A coming of age, a ritual that would never have been
sanctioned by the elders. But after all, it was
the Age of Aquarius and we would soon know much
more than they.

OUR LOVE STORY   John H Galbraith

I remember your laugh,
chuckling in the back of your throat,
your body moving and jiving
in time to the image in your mind.
I remember your eyes,
brimming with tears
when you couldn't help
someone in need.
I remember how we talked,
made promises we couldn't keep.
You held my hand and the room
became smaller each time we met.
I remember how you fell in love
with a different dream.
I remember how we parted
and I tiptoed away.
I remember…

WEDDING ALBUM   John H Galbraith

I hoard the past; photographs,
bills, letters, journals, magazines,
things that were important to me.
Raking through the paper mountain
of thirty years ago I come across
a photograph of our wedding.
How strong we stood, side by side,
you were so young, slender, graceful.
Beautiful in that long gown of white lace,
the sight of you stunned me breathless.
Through the years, we left our City,
reared children, made a home together.
We had common needs that slowly changed,
you wanted one life, I another.
Day after day we drained our love, lost our dreams.
We lived together, eating away at each other.
Until the divorce.

I put the picture in my desk drawer.
Maybe someday we shall get together,
Talk about what went wrong.

BROKEN LEAVES   John Mc Guckin

Walking through the deserted landscape of my mind
I find myself wishing for one more day.
One more moment to be at peace with you.
Simple moments when we strolled and hugged.
Sunlight easing its way through the branches of trees
casting shadows on broken leaves.

Arm in arm we spoke quietly to one another.
I now realize that I never once said I love you.
Always hiding from what?
Imagined slights and hurts.

This is where I end up.
Wishing for one more day with you to tell you I love you,
Knowing now, that had I held you and asked do you love
me, we might be together.
Instead here I end, kicking my way through broken leaves.
The sunlight casting shadows as it tears my heart apart.

I'm lost in those shadows as I think of you.
All I had to do was say I love you.
I think often of those words,
Simple to utter but complex in their simplicity.

All I needed was courage, courage to say I love you –
Would I still be kicking my way through broken leaves
Would I still be wishing for that elusive,

one more day with you.

ALWAYS   John Mc Guckin

It's past, but the past remains alive.
Love is never extinguished by time.
What was true once, remains alive
and vibrant - one glance, one smell
can and does bring memories to life.

I look beyond my days, trying hard to
forget the events that once lived within
my heart, though, as mentioned, it's in
our past where we see our future living.
Today is as much our yesterday, we dream.

What is a minute, or an hour? Only a moment
that still lives within us. Love once lived can
never be forgotten, only wrapped up in memory.
We are part always of what was and can be again.
The past remains alive forever pulsing within.

AN UNFORGETTABLE EXPERIENCE

Kate Glackin

Some years ago my friend Adrienne phoned me on a wet, miserable winter evening.

'Do you fancy a week in the sun, say mid-June, in Tenerife?'I said yes, without hesitation.

"Okay," she said. "I'll book it, pay for it and let you know the details later."

I was elated. I hadn't been abroad since my husband died some years before of a heart attack in Maysfield swimming pool. I was still sad and lonely, still missing him. Perhaps this invitation was just what I needed to lift my spirits, a week in the sun with the best of company.

Two weeks later Adrienne phoned me.

"Good news, all is in order, a self-catering hotel with a verandah overlooking the beach. I've got a better deal in the Algarve. Isn't that wonderful?"

My heart sank. We had spent ten consecutive years holidaying in our villa in the Algarve. Too many happy memories of our life together.

Adrienne went on, "I promise you we'll have a good break. Albufeira is an exciting little town, a beautiful spot."

I screamed out, "Not Albufeira! That's where we had our villa! Please, cancel me out!"

"I'm sorry, I can't do that, it's all paid for and flights confirmed."

I was devastated.

On the morning of our flight to Faro I sat on the plane, sad and lonely. Adrienne was raring to go, full of joy. She looked over at me and said, "Relax, I promise it will do you good."

Just as we became airborne, the young man sitting beside me looked in my direction several times and asked, gently, "Excuse me, I know you. Do you recognise me?"

I looked at him, surprised and said, "I have never seen you before."

He said sadly, "Yes you have. I was the lifeguard on duty in Maysfield swimming pool the morning your husband took his heart attack. I jumped in and tried to resuscitate him before the paramedics arrived. Without success." His voice quivered. "I am so sorry."

I was shocked. I looked into this stranger's face and saw the sadness in his eyes. The woman on the other side of him leaned over to me and took my hand.

"My husband was so upset after that. He so wished he could have saved your husband's life. Telling you his story has closed the book for him."

I looked at them both and stumbled over the words, "But you weren't to blame. My husband had a heart condition, had undergone heart surgery and that was the cause of his death." I sat there, silently weeping.

I felt weak and stunned. Of all the passengers on that packed flight to Portugal (where I didn't want to go), that this man should sit down beside me and relive the whole fatal accident... It was extraordinary, more than a coincidence. To this day I can hardly believe how it could have happened.

We parted quietly when we left the plane and I never saw him again. I felt that my heart had lifted. And when we arrived in Albufeira I could feel my husband's presence the whole time, whispering in my ear: "I will always be with you, always love you."

TOUCHING SHADOWS

Diane Weiner

Nearly.
Drifting and shifting
I see your face
I hear your voice
Then you are gone
Unreachable
To no man's land
Where only the ghosts
Can see and hear
And I am alone again.

HISTORY   Marjorie Jardine

The train arrives in a few minutes. I just can't find the words to express what is wrong with me.

It's too late. You are on the train leaning out, waiting. Our eyes meet, telling you all you need to know. The train is moving away, I can see you leaning out the window, then slowly you fade away. It's knowing you care, knowing each other, then having to part.

My lovely holiday romance…

UNCOUPLED   Gerry McCool

Alas, now we languish in overgrown sidings
Lolling, two pieces of old, rolling stock.
An old engine puffs by, we were once hook and eye
The fire and the steam, now all but a dream.
We could never untangle that rusty triangle
It was all very subtle, I've been told we uncoupled.

AFAR

John H Galbraith

From a distance I watched
you walk slowly towards me.
Each step was a token of your love,
you smiled and outshone the Sun.
In my head I heard the sweetness
of your voice and there was magic
as your lips met mine.
But it was only a dream
of the love that was lost.

I MARRIED MYSELF AT CHRISTMAS

Diane Weiner

It started with the ring – well actually two rings. I went into a store to buy some costume jewellery, bit of bling for Christmas, as you do. I chose a bobby dazzler of a ring. Then the assistant told me it was part of a set of two – Wedding and Engagement. Just for fun I decided to try them on. They really looked good.

The problem was, neither of us could get them off. The assistant assured me she had a solution. After disappearing for some minutes she returned with a phial of oil which she applied liberally to my finger, to no avail as the rings remained stuck fast to my finger.

What could I say except, "I'll take them." That's when I decided to marry myself. Well it's been a long time since I had a decent offer.

Being married has had its ups and downs. It has been a struggle. I have argued constantly with myself, stopped speaking to myself and even cursed myself. I have even fought with myself over the duvet. I have wanted to disown myself, but without taking drastic measures. This has proven very difficult.

Marrying yourself means a lot of soul searching and acceptance of who and what you are. However, I am gradually learning to live with myself. It's definitely easier travelling solo!

FORTY WINKS

Marjorie Jardine

I'm a spritely wee widow
Around forty plus Vat,
You can catch me online
For a bit of a chat.
You could be outnumbered –
I'm a bit of a dame,
So just sling your bow
And I'll tell you my name.
www.xxx

Over to You

- What is your love story?

A love story can be about any relationship with a strong attachment – not just a romantic one. Is there a special person/ pet/ friend in your life, or in your memory?

- Do you have a strong memory of any of these?
  - A first kiss
  - Being somewhere together
  - Your Wedding Day
  - Being let down
  - Losing someone you love

- Have you experienced a strange coincidence?

  What happened, in your own words?
  Sometimes true stories are stranger than fiction – you couldn't make it up!

MORNING GLORY
The Natural World

MORNING GLORY   **Sue McCrory**

It is early
    no visitors yet to the garden.
The piercing sun streams
    through the kitchen window.

A tap drips
    ever so slowly
    in the quiet.

Each drop
    transforms
        in the light
to a sparkling
    white diamond
        in my sink.
I drink it in
    the beauty
        of this morning.

OUR SHANGRI-LA   Diane Weiner

When I was a child growing up in Chamberlain Street in East Belfast, the only flowers we ever saw were the plastic ones which adorned the windows of every house in the street.

We never felt deprived, because as soon as Spring arrived we got on a Belmont Road bus to the "Glens." I can still hear the swish of the branches brushing against the windows as it rounded the corners of the leafy avenues. Each house had a garden filled with flowers, usually roses.

Once at our destination, we left behind the sound of the Shipyard, the narrow streets, and the kitchen houses of East Belfast. We lost the smell of the Connswater, the Ropeworks and the smoke of our industrial city and its linen mills.

We proceeded to explore our surroundings. Silence. Grass growing tall, wild flowers, tall trees, birdsong. Nature at its best. The air so fresh. I can still smell it.

My favourite place was what we called the bluebell glen. We sat there and ate our "piece", usually bread and jam. A feast.

One time we discovered a little stream which we crossed, balancing on the trunk of a tree that had fallen across it. We stopped to dip our toes in the cool, clean water. We made daisy chains, blew the tops off dandelions, held buttercups under each other's chins. Later we would trudge home on tired little legs carrying our trophies, a bunch of bluebells for Mother.

The "Glens" are long gone now, replaced by concrete and motorways. Our small kitchen houses have been knocked down and the industrial giants of my childhood are no more, but my memories of that happy place will always stay with me.

NATURE BOY   John H Galbraith

I was never interested in nature,
in school if we talked about it
we soon found ourselves alone.
Yet it was all around us.
Ormeau Park was twenty minutes' walk
from my front door. Gran got her fresh veg
from the plots in Millar Street.
Every week cows were driven
along the Albertbridge Road
to Saint George's Market.

My inner city primary school
didn't dwell much on the Nature poets.
They didn't dwell much on any poet.
On rare occasions we
were exposed to Wordsworth's
daffodils and Robbie Burns' rose.

To city kids the teacher was speaking
in tongues. We did not want to know
about paintings, poetry or the like.
But we could see the grass growing
between the paving stones of the street.
We knew when the apples and pears
would be ripe in Strandtown orchards.

We could take our treasured cased ball
to Victoria Park. Perhaps pluck those
flowers we read about, but never discussed.

BEFORE LIGHT   Denis Hyde

It was still dark and I couldn't get back to sleep. So, feeling curious what it was like outside in the dark, I opened my blind.

The night sky was bursting with bright stars! And Venus looked like a big light-bulb burning all through the night.

I didn't get back to sleep but I enjoyed my night-time view.

BLUEBELLS

Myra Gibson

They sit in a vase, not caring
what we think of them.
True blue and smelly,
each petal tells its
own story, each green
leaf different from the rest.
Why have they been plucked?
Who took them from the woods?
Who brought beauty to this room?

I KNOW WHY

Myra Gibson

I know why the bluebells bloom,
in crowded masses,

in vivid sky blue shades,
in secret woods and glens

over the earth, by green trees
and fern-like grasses.

Their undiminished glow
pierces the eye and sends

a scene of nature's beauty
that quickly passes

through the broken sunlight
and into higher realms.

A myriad of bluebells
one glorious vision.

Alone, one sad flower,
pines into oblivion.

A CONSEQUENCE OF DEFORESTATION

Sue McCrory

The tall forest trees on the property next to my garden have been pruned. My forest view has altered.

The squirrels have disappeared. I miss them. I keep looking for them. They were so amusing, skimming up the trees, walking along the high fence. One little one would even come up to the kitchen door and sit up straight on his hind feet, in no hurry to leave.

Time has passed. What a surprise. One little squirrel comes walking along the fence, then onto the grass. He hops about for a bit, having a good look round. The other two have not returned. But I am so thankful that one visits now and then. I wonder where the other two have gone.

Early one morning, looking out on the garden, I spot a squirrel walking along the fence. He stops, vigorously shaking his tail like a ra-ra dancer. Next he sits up straight, pausing perhaps, for a rest. Then onto the grass, hunting under bushes, looking for last year's nuts. Next he hops along to the patio and away.

A week passes. And again he comes back for a visit. I wonder if he knows how much I look forward to him dropping by.

LUNAR ECLIPSE, 14th NOVEMBER 2016

Sue McCrory

9.15am: The sky grew darker.

9.30am: A huge, oval shape, like the heart of a furnace. So bright it hurt my eyes, although I only looked for a few seconds. Outside everything went quiet. No birds. No squirrels. No dogs. Not a sound.

9.45am: The sun came back to its normal self. The birds didn't return.

One or two came fluttering back the following day. It took time for everything to return to normal. How lucky to have witnessed this.

HEDGEROWS   John Mc Guckin

Remembering sights and sounds of long ago,
My thoughts drift to old laneways and hedgerows:
honeysuckle, primroses, blackbirds trilling
their sweet songs in idyllic lazy days.

Scrambling around the farmer's feet as he swept
his scythe, cutting the corn, readying it for the miller.
Sheaves bound with a single stalk of corn, fields
of collapsed gold, time passes but memories remain.

Shire horses noble and strong, straining to pull
orange coloured carts loaded with hay –
those singular moments, lying atop the hay –
all so long ago, seems like yesterday.

PINK CHERRY BLOSSOM – FALLEN

Myra Gibson

Pink fragile flowers lying on the ground,
Leaving lonely trees to languish around.
Flowers tossed up in windy disarray,
Homeless leaves scattered over the spring day.

Happy are those who fall in the arbour,
Sheltered, safe from the spring shower.
Till flood water seeks out their rootless graves,
Soaked in the slush their life soon fades.

Lift flowers in your hands, put in a bowl,
Saving them for a while, in your control.
A short time and they are gone, pink glow lost,
Thrown into compost where dead leaves are tossed.

Our lives like flowers, will not last forever,
Beauty fades away, the heart will sever.
I look to the trees without their pink lustre,
To grow back next spring, new pale pink clusters.

SUMMER'S SONG   Myra Gibson

Spring's wayward song fades, now that summer has begun.
All nature sings in harmony to greet the sun,
She sends her warmth and light to shake the struggling roots,
She moves the stubborn soil to caress young shoots.

The sun and earth duet into one summer song.
A lonely skylark singing takes his voice along
With the gentle breeze to join in the joyful throng,
Soaring in highest realms, his solo piercing, long.

Streaks of sunlight through the woods, fall on the flowers.
Bluebells moved by her heat, hum gently for hours.
The violet struggles upwards to catch the light,
Her small, soft voice singing a melody so bright.

Autumnal winds soon bluster through warm, summer air.
Leaves desert the trees, gliding over everywhere.
A lonely walker passing treads the faded heaps,
Rustling into echoes as Summer falls asleep.

Winter follows, freezing Autumn into retreat.
All too soon, time takes away Summer's dancing feet.
Now the song of Winter comes sonorous and long,
In my dreams I still hear Summer's opulent song.

AUTUMN LEAVES   Myra Gibson

Leaves growing, living on the maple tree
Young and vibrant for all to see
Happy and content with their friends
Safe and secure until Summer ends.

Now it is Autumn you are fading
Fragile as you fall gliding
Down into dark heaps forsaken
Waiting for Autumn breezes to awaken.

The maple tree stands forlorn and alone
Winds blowing her leaves far from home
Faded leaves with faded colours
Of red, yellow, and golden orange.

A COLD SNAP

Denis Hyde

Cold cold day.
Jack Frost has done his work,
scattered frost all over the grass.

Hear it crunching underfoot,
the clothes on the washing line frozen stiff,
the pavement a skating rink to slip and slide on.

The morning sun comes gleaming,
beams on brittle Jack.
he groans and is gone – just like that!

ROAD ACCIDENT

Myra Gibson

A roofless lorry on a busy road
Shakes its slithered cargo of silent heaps.
Shining bodies swell as they try to gasp
For one last, futile, dry, communal breath.
A sudden crash and all are hurled with force
Into a waterless field, crushed and dead.
Thousands of mackerel, their glazed, sightless eyes
Staring up at a bright, remorseless sun.
Silent silver shoals stolen,
From squalling sonorous seas

A MERCURIAL MOMENT   **Myra Gibson**

The heron stands, silent, searching
On a wooden plinth protruding
From the river's swampy shallows.
He sees rhythmic ripples spreading
Round a silver shape swimming.
Diving off his stand with purpose
In one mercurial moment
A silver fish is swallowed.

THE PROMONTARY   Gerry McCool

It won't give in without a fight.

The sea steals away the land on either side,

Ribboned wracks of seaweed mark out the battle line.

The promontory though, consists of igneous strata.

Used as a defensive stronghold long ago,

Steep cliffs protected people on three sides,

The land approach controlled by palisades.

Within the fort, the kiss of history is narcotic

The edge of the continent, a numinous emotion

This Atlantic coast, in turn brutal, then angelic

The swaying whoosh of waves from down below

The pebbles scramble after the sniggering surf

This promontory refuses to demote to a mere sea-stack –

It won't give in without a fight.

LEAVING THE SHORE   Myra Gibson

Gentle waves lapping over my feet,
As I stand on a shallow shore.
Gentle waves ebbing a rippling retreat
To meet the sea once more.

Gentle rays of sunshine warming all
As I stand on a wave-bereft floor.
Gentle rays trapped in cloudy enthral,
Disappear from sky and shore.

Standing here alone with the tide out far,
The sun veiled in a cloudy grey sky.
I must depart from my gentle shore,
Distant waves, distant sun goodbye.

WHAT IS BEAUTY?   Myra Gibson

A rainbow curving over
the sky, wraps its magic
round the earth below, in
a parcel of coloured glow

brightening the eye, uplifting the soul

after the grey, dark, lonesome,
rain-soaked morning.

Over to You

- What do you see out your window?
Do you feed the birds or watch the sun setting?

- What are your memories of school outings,
the nature table, the countryside?

- Have you ever watched an eclipse? Or been
in a thunderstorm or flood? Was it frightening?
What did you see, hear, smell, taste, feel?

- Do you feel close to Nature? Is there a view, a
season – a particular place or tree – that brings you joy or
comfort?

+

ADJUSTING
Changing Times

ADJUSTING   **Bernice Burrows**

It is Fall, everything is changing.
As much as I dislike this,
it is a necessary step –

Change isn't all bad,
or so I'm told.
I will do what I've always done – adjust.

Do what's necessary. But
life shouldn't be only about the necessary,
It should be lived to the full.

After Fall, Winter.
I examine the leaves where they have fallen,
like a forensic policewoman.

I walk in the Park,
Watch, listen, cry,
Raise my head and smile.

After Fall, Winter.
Adjust, talk, write, wait –
For, after Winter, Light.

GONE   John H Galbraith

The Woodstock and the Albert have fallen
to the thud of the developers' hammer.
Gone are the shops and pubs of the fifties;
no longer can we call at Harry James' fish shop
to buy a bag of dulse, whelks or potted herring.
We can't give a shout at Hugh Gemmel's pork shop
for pigs' feet, ham-nabs or a pork pie.
Holy Joe isn't able to lead us gently from his pub
after our third pint of stout.
The doors of the Plough, the Primrose Inn and the Tramway
bar are closed; pubs don't sell
hard boiled eggs or three keg Guinness now.
Stevie's shop isn't there to sell penny Woodbine,
Frankenstein's monster has stopped haunting
the Picturedrome, the Winkie and the Ambassador.
Bulldozers have swallowed the Woodstock and
the Albert. Progress has arrived
with the stroke of the draftsman's pen.

THE LOVE OF MY LIFE   **Marjory Jardine**

This house in my memory,
Instilled in my mind,
Will be with me forever
Whatever befalls.
With joy and with sorrow
That evening dawned –
The end of an era
Love's old sweet song

MOVING ON   Marjory Jardine

Life was an everlasting adventure where I was born and brought up surrounded by lots of friends in a mixed area in the county of Armagh. With just having a brother I was lost for company until I got to know the Brady family, with a household of seven children or so. We would have supper together, say daily prayers together and at Christmas visited their chapel to pay our respects. Politics was indeed a foreign word.

During these tender years of my life, my family became friendly with a widow lady, Mrs Elliot. She had married and moved to Dublin where sadly she lost her husband. She then returned to her home town and became a lodger in her former home. Later the family who occupied the house left for Belfast and she reclaimed her beloved home. But she wasn't entitled to a pension so she took in lodgers and did tailoring to keep afloat. It was at this point that she became acquainted with my parents and she became part of my life.

Then my parents made a move to the city of Belfast, which I hated, so I went back to stay with my seven cousins who had been left orphaned. I often visited Mrs Elliott who was always pleased to see me and I spent many happy hours in her house.

Gradually over the years my Brady family friends left for Canada and I married. Changes all round. I continued to keep in touch with my widow friend and often went to see her at weekends and helped her with the upkeep of her house. Then in early 1970 she passed away quite suddenly.

Her lovely house was taken over by strangers. It was the saddest day in my life saying goodbye to this place of happy memories. Needless to say, a quiet drive to my old town allows me a peep at that beloved house where I had been made so welcome.

WHAT DO YOU MISS?   Sue McCrory

I miss riding my bicycle.
I miss the local post office.
I miss ballroom dancing
And singing solo.
I miss my old, comfy shoes,
Going to the races
And going to America.
I miss some of my old neighbours,
I miss the seaside,
I miss the dog,
I miss Santa…

MY FAVOURITE CUP   Denis Hyde

I had a favourite cup for donkey's years.
It was bone china.
One day I opened the cupboard
And found it broken in pieces.
I have other cups but this one –
It was my mum's cup and special.
I still have others,
But not like my mum's cup.

CHRISTMAS PRESENTS   Sue McCrory

Many years ago when I was a child, my family were very lucky to get a turkey for Christmas. My father plucked its feathers until it was bare, then Mother washed it and cooked it in the three burner oil cooker.

Father Christmas left me an apple, an orange, a few sweets, gob stoppers, liquorice sticks, a game of Ludo and a game of Snakes and Ladders. There were crayons, a basket of nectarines and a colouring-in book, two hankies and a pair of socks.

All were put into a silk stocking that my mother had hung at the side of the fireplace. Father Christmas was left a piece of bread and cheese and the reindeer some carrots. I was completely satisfied with all the wonderful things that he had left me and on Christmas morning I posted a thank you letter up the chimney.

Sitting here and looking at what my grandchildren have received, it appears that they got a lot. (Father Christmas and his elves must be working their socks off all year round.)

CHRISTMAS CLUB   Gerry McCool

'Our Christmas Club now open.'
Sure you haven't got a hope in
Getting those younger folks today
Into that old fashioned way,
Putting money down up front
For some mystic future want.
Or would they ever understand
That the money in their hand
Would buy presents for everybody
That would be paid for already.
What a strange concept to endure
To pay for things before they're yours.
No. We don't do that anymore.
I'll just check my credit score.
Yes, last year's Christmas splendour
Will be paid off by November.
So, I can plan a splurge again
To be paid off God knows when.
Yes, I'm ready for more banter
With my Gold card, good old Santa!

CORRESPONDENTS   Denis Hyde

My mum used to get letters from her sister and cousin, beautifully written by hand in fountain pen, on Basildon Bond (the posh velum). They both wrote extraordinarily long letters, maybe four pages, with no space left for another word, crammed into the corners and sideways on - so much news to tell.

Both correspondents are gone. We don't get handwritten letters landing on our doormat anymore.

A DIFFERENT ERA

Sue McCrory

It was a Wednesday in the middle of winter. I was lying on the delivery table in the Jubilee Hospital. The time was 9am and I had just given birth to a baby boy, my son. The midwife took the baby to get him cleaned up and then I held him for the first time – the most wonderful feeling in the world! I felt so relieved after all the hard work. All was well.

I asked the staff, "Do any of you smoke?" One nurse nodded and I asked her for a cigarette and a light.

Still on the delivery table, I smoked the whole cigarette. I felt great. I stubbed the tip out and skipped off the table to go for a shower.

Can you imagine that happening today?

KILWEE, THE YELLOW CHURCH Gerry McCool

The Yellow Church, I can see its thatch and wattles
Known only by its flattened Anglo name now.
Thirteen centuries of weather and denudation
New homes to be built here for a newer people.
To find a footprint of a sacred building
Two weeks to rescue all that might remain.

Powered by clan chieftains, newly converted
Clerics from that same ennobled family
New bards and priests succeeding age old Druids.
Patrick a remnant from the ruling Romans
Captured in a raid by Irish rovers,
A herdsman slave up on pagan Slemish.

And Columba, himself close to the High King's clan,
Sailed to spread the word from blessed Iona,
A band of tribal Scotii from Dalriada,
To a country that still bears their name today.
Then on down south to the pagan Anglo-Saxons
To Cuthbert and his new church at Lindisfarne.

Found, two stone fragments from a Celtic high cross
That may throw light on their primary purpose
Before books, the pictures carved in stone –

Didactic, for an unread congregation.
Stories that were centuries old already
Reflect events in far off alien lands.

No building stone, just fresh wood and wattles,
Two lines of dark postholes in the lighter soil
Supported the golden thatch well seen from far-off
No Romanesque nor Corinthian columns;
Enlightenment with only rushlight torches...
I gazed up through the blowing branches
And thought I saw the son of a carpenter, smile.

THE PHONE BOX   Gerry McCool

When the phone box was broken, we had to wait for the pub to open
Or get a bus or a taxi to talk with someone.
You might be too late or early, there was no way of knowing
And the day could be wasted, by the time you were done.

Now things have moved on, and cell phones abound
Communication is instant, you can always be found
You dare not forget it wherever you go
Why did you not answer they all want to know?

Big Brother had nothing on these little critters
There's hi-fi, then wi-fi, and facebook and twitter
No need for writing, or letters, or stamps
Keep up with your e-mail, leave nothing to chance

The banks are all closing, you can do it online,
Manage debts and pay bills, it's your own chance to shine!
If you know just nine numbers, you can be your own boss
And watch columns of zeros march across and across.

Now, could I find me a phone box, they're almost extinct
How to work the dammed thing, I blinked and I blinked
Ten pence for three minutes, I seemed to recall
Now one seventy-five to make that same call!

Rang my brother in Melbourne on this new thing called Skype
A technological miracle if you believe all the hype
You can look at each other while talking away
God you've piled a few stone on and your hair is so gray

Now when I call them my camera's not on
I'm fed up with these Aussies, so slim and so bronzed
I'll go back to my letters, I can still read and write
But there's so much to say, it takes you all night.

A MILE APART   Gerry McCool

We used to visit the Shankill Road when we were young,
My mother always used to say the shops were better there.
The landmarks were Clonard Monastery, and the Stadium cinema.
There were no peace walls then, or wondering if it was okay
where you were.

Cupar Street ran from the Shankill to the Falls,
A mile long litmus paper that might change from green to orange.
Today both marked by memorial gardens for locals
Who had fallen in a Christian war, not even foreign.

I had been to Berlin but never to Berlin Street,
Ironically Shankill itself, a reminder of its Gaelic past.
No memorials or painted pavements, in Malone or Helen's Bay
Why just in the poor streets of Falls and Shankill, should it last?

For people who live in Nottingham, Nebraska, or Nepal
Would they really see much difference between the Shankill
and the Falls?

A LAST GOODBYE   Marjorie Jardine

I looked around and there you were,
A treasured scene but now no more.
The time is ripe, the dust has set
Your smiling features on the shelf.
A last goodbye with no regret,
This final couplet in our song
I guess it's time for moving on.

THE HAUNTED HOUSE   Gerry McCool

I have seen her there –
Not in a house in a dark forest,
Isolated, tangled up in overgrowth
With little square windows,
That bode an odd uneasiness.
Still, this house was haunted
By an absence, not a presence.
Someone who never lived there,
Roaming from room to room.
Frightening perhaps, this entity.
I will take that chance –
Please, please darken my door.

THE OLD MAN AND THE YOUNG CROW

Myra Gibson

The old man stands quietly, watching.
Through the window he sees a young crow
struggling with a broken wing unable to fly.

The old man's memory is riddled with age.
It has confused his life. He is trapped in a cage
but is still capable of feeding the crow.

He has a garden of trees and many flowers
where the birds of the area fly for hours.
It is a haven for all his feathered friends.

My brother lives in a home far from his home.
Will his garden be dug over and become stone?
Will his birds fly away along with the young crow?

I don't know.

BETTY'S STORY   Diane Weiner

As she walked up the winding path, tottering on her stilettos and wearing a very short, tight skirt, she felt triumphant.

She had fought a long, lonely battle to reach this point. Fought the bureaucrats and won, disregarded the advice of almost everyone and pushed aside her own fears and misgivings. Now her moment had come, something was about to happen – and whatever the outcome, it would change her life forever. Change a life of abuse, physical and mental, suffered at the hands of her adoptive parents. Her life had been hell but she was a survivor with a determination that no-one, nothing could shake.

As she rounded a bend, the house came into view. She took a sharp intake of breath. Situated in an elevated position, surrounded by beautiful gardens, it was imposing, large, expensive, posh. She thought of the dreary little kitchen house that she had grown up in, but she felt no bitterness. That was not why she was here.

As she reached the door she paused for just a second, straightened her shoulders, held her head high and rang the bell. A shadow appeared and the door opened. It was her. It was like looking in a mirror.

Betty had found her mother.

Over to You

- What buildings have gone from your area?
  Tell us about one that is part of your past.

- Did you ever revisit a special place to find it had changed, was quite different from how you remembered it?

- What do you miss?
  What do you not miss!

- What was the best present you ever got from Santa?
  How have things changed for children today?

- Remember when there were hardly any TVs or phones? How did we manage?

- What would you like to change, if you could?

BEFORE I KNEW
Reflections

BEFORE I KNEW   Gerry McCool

Before I knew that this life could only be lived one day at a time
I thought that everyone but me had their lives planned out in an
orderly sequence.

Before I knew that diamonds were forever
I let many gemstones slip between my fingers.

Before I knew a little about love, I knew lots about lust.

Before I knew that many in authority were liars, thieves, or worse
I thought they had been entrusted to look after the rest of us.

Before I knew about self-will or resentment
I blamed my guardian angel for being away somewhere when I
needed him most.

Before I knew this universe was thirteen billion years old
I thought history began with Henry VII in 1485.

Before I knew about the spirit and creator of the universe
I thought that God was just a picture that was painted on a board.

ANGELS   Gerry McCool

My guardian angel is leaving in disgrace
He said I wasn't part of this human race
He roared I'd worn him out, he'd have to go
If he hung round me anymore, we'd both go down below.
I thought 'Oh God, how will I ever survive
Without this guy who kept my soul alive.'
He said 'Quit your low down ways and start anew'
And I'll search the depths of heaven for another saviour that might do.
So I changed my sinful ways and became quite good
And God rewarded me in a way only he could.
I thought nothing more could surprise me in this world
But my new guardian angel, incredibly, was a girl.
She shimmered like a Marian visitation,
Calmed the storms of my wild imagination.

How could I be bad with this chick watching out?
Yeah, she'd take the good out of being bad, I didn't doubt.
Embarrassment would keep me on my toes
I'd be no longer lonely, out there counting crows.
I'd stroll along the road such a happy loon
When I'd see her face above I'd begin to swoon.
The stress of being so saintly, then took its toll
It raised a daily conflict in my soul.
She'd shake her head each time I'd jump the rails

Sometimes I gurned I'd be better off in jail.
I thought I'd go back and try a new direction,
Maybe spiritual progress, not spiritual perfection.
This guardian lady's great but not much craic,
If I'd to pick one or the other, think I'd take my old guy back.

I DON'T WANT TO LOSE...   Gerry McCool

I don't want to lose my sanity again
Be scorched by that blowtorch blue flame
Be late, or miss all my trains.

I don't want to lose my willingness to try
For those who know on me they can rely
Just like the North Star in the sky.

I don't want to lose touch with that great power
Right through every waking hour
Or thought for those who never flower.

I don't want to lose that non-voracity for greed
Just asking only what I need
In all thought and word and deed.

I don't want to lose, my capacity for life
With all the problems and the strife
Make sure wrong's still worse than right.

MY REFLECTION ON A BAD DAY Jackie Taylor

Life shone a light on my reflection
And I saw my cracks, my flaws,
The weariness of freshness dimmed,
The emptiness of a vacuum
That nature abhors
And I cried and cried,
Spilling out my sorrow
Into the void and I reflected on a life
Long unfilled with comfort,
Light and love.

MY REFLECTION ON A GOOD EVENING

Jackie Taylor

Life shone a light on my reflection
And laughter filled the air.
I danced the rhythm of my bones
I didn't have a care.
Music filled my very soul
I flipped the coin from tails to heads
And went the extra mile
There was no effort in the glitter ball
Of my happy success
And in that moment I really knew
I'd settle for nothing less
Than me, me at my best!

OLD HABITS

Denis Hyde

I have a habit of speaking too quickly.
I try to slow down and stay calm
But often people think I talk
In a foreign language.
I am aware that I need to slow down.
I'm trying, but I don't think
I'll be able to break the habit –
Life is just too short.

ENOUGH

Jackie Taylor

Can it just be enough
That I've made it here today
I can just listen
Can't think of things to say
The world is just a buzz
I want to get away.

MAYBE

Marjory Jardine

When you're feeling low, when you're feeling flat
Meet up with old friends that make you laugh
For friends are the tonic that works the best
That does not have any side effects.

What could be missing that could be put right
This world with its beauty, in nature's delights,
A harvest of plenty is there at a touch –
Maybe, just maybe, we're asking too much.

ARCHIMEDES' CROW   Gerry McCool

Perched up on the pitcher's rim,
He pondered this predicament:
Plenty of water in the old cream jug,
But how could he take refreshment?

The neck of the jug was much too slim,
For him to get down for a drink.
Standing there on the farmyard step,
He would have to step back and think.

The unreachable water down below,
Flashed up a mocking reflection.
His friend the red robin watched from close by
With a sure, but querulous expression.

Well if it takes me all day, I must find a way,
To solve this intractable problem.
It is too hot and dry, and two miles to fly
Down to the stream at Ben Bulben.

An old memory returned then to his young corbie mind;
When a fledgling he'd had a problem of a similar kind
His mother was showing him how to bathe and get clean
But there was not enough water to shake and then preen.

So she placed in the puddle some pebbles and things
And soon the cold water was up to his wings!
Perhaps that idea could work again on this day
He would set about trying it out right away.

He searched the farmyard for what could be found,
There were nice purple pebbles just scattered around.
He brought six or seven back round to the jug
Dropped them into the water and heard them glug-glug.

When the ripples calmed down he got such a shock –
The water had risen right up to the top!
He drank the cool liquid with a satisfied smile
His friend the red robin, he'd known all the while.

RULER   John Mc Guckin

Started work at the bricklaying.
Okay, thought I, what do I need?
Have to ask, hadn't a clue what to do.
Anyway, said to this guy,
Where do I get a ruler?
Already had a bat and ball –
okay, today that's known as a level.

But then, ah heck, where was I?
Oh yeah, looking for this ruler.
Finally got one in a pawn shop on
the Old Lodge Road. Little did
I think that the ruler would become
as obsolete as the road I bought it on
(the feet and inches on both sides
of the ruler, that is).

It was 1962, hadn't heard of metric,
perhaps decimals in school.
Anyway, the dopey ruler was superseded
by, wait for it, a blooming tape measure
with only metric on it. Most important tool
in the game, the ruler – ach heck, yes,
the tape as well.

First thing you learn is: always measure
down when you're building up.
Had to finally admit the tape was handier,
but still the auld rule remains at home
to this day.
Both it and myself are obsolete,
though the intervening years - between myself,
ruler and tape - were times to be cherished.

IF I RULED THE WORLD Diane Weiner

I would be 29, blond, beautiful, wear size 4 shoes and have a degree in Rocket Science.

I would be a cross between Mother Teresa and Marilyn Monroe.

I would be able to read Men's minds but I still wouldn't understand them and I would disregard every single word that came out of their mouths.

In my world every woman would have the gift of at least one child regardless of age or status. These children would speak only words of endearment. The "F" word would be forever banned. They would grow up in a safe and happy environment free from hurt, hunger, pain and prejudice.

Doctors would never make mistakes.

Politicians would make great decisions and create a good life for all.

Each person would be given a piece of land to call their own. Every house would be the same, no keeping up with the Jones.

Mankind would be filled with love and compassion for each and every fellow human being.

And finally, if I ruled the world, my hairdresser would never ever say, "Take your wee glasses off, love."

WALL   John Mc Guckin

Granite, bluestone, hod, cement
building bricks, scaffolding, ladder, planks
muckboard, shovel, trowel - and don't forget
the jointer and line pin -
                    now we will start building.

Keep the wall plumb, don't let it go hard or soft,
most of all, remember it's for the person who's paying,
so do the right thing - leave it as good as you would for yourself.
Don't fear the tallyman or let mistakes make you frown -
keep on top of the wall mentally and you'll win hands down.
It's easy to say, ach to heck with it, but remember
you need to put bread on the table.
The wall pays the way forward.

THE TAXI DRIVER   Kate Glackin

The taxi arrived twenty minutes late.

"What kept you?" I said angrily to the driver. "Your office told me you left forty minutes ago, I have a flight to catch to London."

The taxi driver was very contrite.

"I'm really sorry," he said. "I felt a bit unwell this morning, I think it is indigestion, but don't worry it will pass."

I said happily that I was off to London for the week-end with some of my old school friends and asked him to please drive fast to the airport because I wanted to be in good time for a cuppa with them and wander round the duty-free shop.

He never said a word but I noticed in the mirror that his face was pale and his breathing was loud and rapid. He kept punching his chest with his clenched fist. His driving was erratic.

From the back seat I shouted, "Are you all right?"

He whispered with difficulty, "I think I'm having a heart attack, please get me to Antrim hospital now. I will direct you."

He stopped at the nearest lay-by and I struggled to push this hefty stranger into the passenger seat.

"I can't do this," I exclaimed.

"Please help me," he said. "I think I'm dying."

I turned the ignition and drove. When we arrived at the A&E he was whisked away immediately. He shouted from the trolley, "Please get my passenger to the airport now, her flight is due to leave soon."

The ambulance driver drove me there with flashing lights and loud horns. We were speeding at what seemed ninety miles per hour. I arrived to hear the final call for my flight to London, I was the last passenger on board.

My friends shouted, "What kept you?" I said it was a long story and sank into my seat, utterly shattered and bewildered.

However, I enjoyed the weekend with my friends and when I arrived home a huge bouquet of flowers and a generous gift voucher were delivered to my door. The card read:

Thank you, my dearest passenger, for saving my life,
Your (late) taxi driver!

ART OF LIFE   John Mc Guckin

To survive art has to be tangible.
Art should state: Here I am, touch me,
caress me, covet me. I'm your heart,
the art of life. In my many forms
I am sought after, despised, copied and
stolen. I am what I am - the art of life.

How you view me is from your
take on life. I live in your heart.
That truth remains inviolate.
My sense of being encircles the globe.
Known as imagination,
I belong to each one of you.

How you pursue me depends on how much of
you is allowed to shine through. Reach out.
Grasp hold of me. I belong in your mind.

Good, bad, or indifferent, use me.
Your imagination decides
how I come to life.
I cannot exist without you.
You are me and I am you,
the art of life.

Over to You

- What were you like when you were wet behind the ears, 'young and foolish' like Gerry

- What do you <u>not</u> want to lose?
  What do you think is 'enough' in life for you?

- At work did you use any tools in particular, like a ruler, a typewriter, a needle, some kind of machine, or were you behind the wheel of a car?

- Have you ever had some unexpected emergency like Kate's with the taxi driver?

- Do you believe in guardian angels? Have you had any experience where you felt that someone was watching over you?

- If you ruled the world, what would you decree? How would your world be?

FORGET ME NOT
Later Days

WHEN I AM OLD   Bernice Burrows

After the poem of the same title by Jenny Joseph

When I am old I shall wear pink ribbons in my hair,
A hearing aid or two
And sing and dance with younger men,
Express my wisdom through the pen.
90 years young, some would say –
I know my dear, I wasn't born yesterday!
You're only as young as you feel.

When I am old I shall ride on merry-go-rounds
And eat sweets and lollipops.
When I am old I shall smoke cigars and smell the flowers
And collect my pension late.
I shall take my magic earrings out when politicians preach.
When I am old I shall roam the streets in flip-flops,
Own a little cat or two, feeding them Irish stew.
I shall stay up late and express my point of view,
I shall travel the world, and see the sea…
But what's secret will stay secret, between you and me.

WHEN I'M CLEANING WINDOWS

Diane Weiner

I have no blinds in my house and rarely draw the curtains. I enjoy looking out the window at the world and suffer the consequences of those at liberty to look in at me. It works fine until the window cleaner makes his monthly visit. He never calls on the same day and often catches me unawares. This man has seen me in all forms of dress and undress over the last twenty years. Let's face it, there are tasks and activities that one would prefer not to be seen doing by others.

I never blush when he calls for payment now. We greet each other with the greatest propriety. I inquire how his wife is and when he is going on his next cruise. He is very polite, asking about the state of my health and exchanging notes about the weather. It's pointless now to change my habits. He's probably tired looking at me anyway, after all this time.

PRE-PENSION YEAR   Gerry McCool

Startled, I wake up in darkness.
Strangely segmented, a cold-blooded moon
shines through the monkey puzzle tree.
Toothed branches against the shining light,
like the stitching on a post-mortem body.
Where had the daylight gone?
A three hour golf round in the air.
A little sit-down in my chair.
Stiff and sore, and fingers cramped.
It was pre-pension year.
Someone had correctly worked this out.
Bed beckons, but the collateral of this sleep already spent -
I must read, or lie awake and wonder
How many more stations before this train gets there.

MY WEEK   Diane Weiner

Monday

An S.O.S from work. Yeah! They still need me!

Tuesday

I nearly got saved in a Gospel Hall in East Belfast. It was at the funeral of a friend's mother. Not entirely a sad occasion as the lady was 95 and had a lovely send-off:
rousing hymns; a great orator giving the tribute; standing room only and a lot of handsome men in smart suits. Hallelujah!

Wednesday

Universally challenged at a quiz in the synagogue where I mingled with the Jewish community.

Thursday

Hairdressers'. A young girl shampooing my hair: "You are lucky to have such thick hair, most old people's hair gets very thin."

Friday

Disturbed two bees mating in mid-air. (Who knew?) They were very cross.

Saturday

Saturday was sinful! I've painted my toenails red in celebration!

Sunday

Morning service at St Anne's Cathedral. I prayed for all. Am turning into a religious zealot!

Today

My cat has taken umbrage, ignoring me in that disdainful way that cats do. Anyone know where I can find a cat whisperer? I've done nothing wrong. Although I do think that all my idle chat and ruminating has finally got on his nerves.

THE CROSSING   Gerry McCool

Back home, familiar, but grey, a nihilism pervades,
Back from that house, that scene, shocking.
Did it happen?
Just a bedside visitor to my sick friend,
But an awful foreboding, in that room.
A family fear, tangible,
A silent beseeching,
A power greater than me was needed here.
But here I was, utilised, absorbed
In those few moments of infinity,
A life ending, a crossing, a family sorrow.
Humanity benefited by his existence.
The grey disperses, still dim, a new dawn breaks,
Renewal beckons to those whose eyes reopen.

AN OCTOGENARIAN'S DREAM

John H Galbraith

Because I am eighty

I shall wear an Elvis wig,
so people will stare
and call me a silly old fool.

I shall put on pink shirts
because they look good,
with my rainbow ties.

I shall put on my blue suede shoes
because they suit my jiving feet,
and they help me twist and shout.

I shall bring out my Teddy Boy gear
because the kids will have some fun
seeing their Granddad in fancy dress.

I shall say hello to everyone
because I'm eighty,
getting older, but still alive.

IT'S HELL TO BE OLD   John H Galbraith

It's Hell to be old
Sitting here in my empty flat
My wife's gone and our old bed's cold.

Everyone has left the fold
There's no mail on my mat
It's Hell to be old.

My life's on hold
Haven't even got a cat
My wife's gone and our old bed's cold.

Woman next door thinks I'm bold
All I wanted was a chat
It's Hell to be old.

Can't drive anymore, the car's sold
Keep getting drunk, I'm turning to fat
My wife's gone and our old bed's cold.

No-one left that I can scold
Family say I'll never make a diplomat
It's Hell to be old.
My wife's gone and our old bed's cold.

FORGET ME NOT Kate Glackin

Please don't ask me questions,
Don't expect me to remember –
> I have lost all that,
> I'm not the same.

Just let me stay quiet, close to you,
Let me hold your hand –
> I can't help the way I am,
> I don't even know my name.

Your face is familiar, like the warmth of the sun.
Your eyes make me feel I belong, but
> I am lost somewhere
> I'm not to blame.

Don't be cross when I repeat myself,
Don't scold me when I'm loud and wrong,
> Look close, the person deep inside
> Will always love you 'till
> The best of her is gone.

HIGH DEPENDENCY   John H Galbraith

The Duchess of Doom slips
into the High Dependency ward.
She moves slowly from bed to bed,
no one sees her, no one hears her.
Gently she probes each patient's strength
asking each one if they will travel with her.
Wee Willy senses her presence,
he smiles as she embraces him,
they sidle out from the ward.
The Life Support machine is silent.

Soon the staff will clear the bed,
prepare it for the next occupant.
This is the reality of life and death
on the High Dependency ward
of Belfast's City Hospital.

CLOSING TIME   John H Galbraith

I knew his death was near.
It was as if a black cloak
was resting on his shoulders.
I remember the last few times
when I saw him. How he stood
in the doorway, his smile lighting up
the darkness of the room.
Just for a frozen moment
he lost twenty years.
I waved at him, my eyes filling,
thinking each time
it would be our last.

OUTSIDE WILTON'S FUNERAL PARLOUR

John H Galbraith

After the funeral service
the mourners gather in the forecourt.
Cigarettes are pulled from packets
and lit with great care.
Soft words, like rustling leaves
are whispered between friends.
They have come to say goodbye
to an old friend but keep saying hello
to people they last saw at a similar place.
The elderly survey the faces around them,
looking for old acquaintances.
They reach out and grasp the hands
of fellow mourners, each one
reluctant to let go of the other.

FRIENDS IN CITY WAY   Marjorie Jardine

What shall we do when all else has gone?
The times when we laughed and cried all done.

The wonderful memories of laughter and tears
Bring back those happy, happy years.

To think of the new friends we have found
So precious they are, when you're up or you're down

It's a gift they accept me with all my frowns,
More precious to me than a great golden crown.

Over to You

- What things will you give yourself permission to do, when (or now) you are old? (Bernice and John had a go at this.)

- What things do you do in a week? Try keeping a diary of what you do in one week. Add a few comments, as Diane did, to give it some spice!

- What do you look forward to? This could be simple, everyday things, like the next cuppa, or a favourite TV programme. Or it could be special things like a trip, a visit from someone close, or something you would really like to do, given the opportunity.

- For you, what is the worst thing about growing old and what is the best thing? John has put his finger on some of the worst things in "It's Hell to be Old."

- How important are friends to you? Try describing a friend you know well – the way he or she speaks, the things she or he does, little sayings or ways of behaving – the things you have been through together, the things that make that person special.

Biographical notes

Bernice Burrows

A keen student who likes reading, Kenco coffee and music – not bad for a deaf woman who likes expressing herself through poetry, going to writing groups and learning new things!

John H Galbraith

A retired Civil Servant living in East Belfast. In 2001 John joined a B.I.F.H.E. (now the Belfast Met) Creative Writing class tutored by Ruth Carr and has been writing ever since. Some poems published in *The Lonely Poet's Guide to Belfast* and further Poetry in Motion anthologies. Founder member of *Words Alive* and currently the Chair.

Myra Gibson

Sang for years in The Performers' Club under the direction of Mr Frank Capper. Myra has penned a few poems in her time, and quite a few more since joining *Words Alive*. She has also enjoyed meeting and making new friends. Published in Poetry in Motion anthologies, *New Belfast* and *Right up There* (New Belfast Community Arts Initiative) and in *A Sense of Place* (United Press).

Kate Glackin

A retired secretary and avid reader, Kate joined the class to express her thoughts and ideas. Enjoys charitable work, the Speakers' Circle, and regularly attends the theatre and concerts of the Ulster Orchestra.

Denis Hyde

A retired warehouse worker with a hearing difficulty since birth, but still engaged in many interests. These include reading, bowls and films. Denis got involved with creative writing since he retired.

Marjorie Jardine

A retired Civil Servant who has always been inspired by the written word. Having joined *Words Alive* in recent years Marjorie has found the experience both encouraging and rewarding.

Gerry McCool

With more time since retirement, Gerry is trying his hand at poetry, writing about everything: from archaeology and lost causes to grandchildren, from Archimedes to Donald Trump.

Sue McCrory

A mother and grandmother. Sue started writing by accident, having attended a *Words Alive* Culture Night event in the library. Delighted to become one of the group, to learn from everyone, listening to their stories and to begin writing her own.

John Mc Guckin

A crusader of personal and political truths. John used to go to the bricklaying in the mornings, then slip upstairs and write a poem. It was a hobby never disclosed. Now, with several books self-published, it's more than a hobby – writing and reading books are a way of life. He has come through a lot, raised a family and is happy to be a part of *Words Alive.*

Jackie Taylor

A jack of all trades, Jackie is a talented painter, writer and singer and has been known to treat the class to a song or two.

Diane Weiner

A semi-retired business woman. Inspired to put pen to paper to capture childhood memories, Diane joined the class and has been encouraged by the support and generosity of fellow members.

217

Ruth Carr

Lives in Belfast where she has worked as a tutor in community education for over 30 years. She had the good fortune to facilitate *Words Alive* creative writing group from inception. With two collections of poetry to her name, *There is a House* and *The Airing Cupboard* (Summer Palace Press) she hopes to have a third out in Autumn 2017.

#0356 - 270317 - C0 - 210/148/12 - PB - DID1795482